Democratic
Administration

PART I CREATIVE MANAGEMENT

PART II DEMOCRACY IN ADMINISTRATION

ORDWAY TEAD

Lecturer in Personnel Administration,
Columbia University. Author of
The Art of Leadership,
New Adventures in Democracy, etc.

ASSOCIATION PRESS

291 Broadway   New York 7, N. Y.

145

Printed in the United States of America

Contents

3

PREFACE

Part I of this book makes again available in slightly revised form the brochure *Creative Management*, first published in 1935. A continuing demand for the text prompts this reissue.

In order to supply a fuller philosophical setting for the democratic practices there set forth, it is now possible to add Part II, written some years later. This second essay seems to me hopefully to set the original theme in a more adequate frame, to show the deeper reasons for the methods earlier offered, and to clarify wider applications and implications.

Together the two Parts—even though they are not the systematic statement on democratic administration as a fine art, which I hope eventually to write—do present a rationale for democratic action of a sensible kind in day-to-day experiences, as to which there is more curiosity and more eagerness for specific guidance than ever before.

Although the initial essay was originally written out of contacts and consultations with social agencies and character-building institutions, the years have shown that it has had a wider interest and usefulness. The second essay, on the other hand, deliberately offers no specific applied examples. It is stated in generalized terms because of my strong conviction that applications of its conclusions can be made to many different types of organized effort. And the discerning reader can readily adapt points of view and methods to his own situation.

What democracy as a way of life requires on its operational side is a matter about which there is alert concern in business, government, and education no less than in philanthropic bodies.

This slender volume is offered as one student's interim report on the what, the why, and the how—in the hope that it may be practically helpful in numerous organizations in various areas of human effort.

Ordway Tead

New York City
April 10, 1945

PART I

CREATIVE MANAGEMENT

INTRODUCTION

When new organizations first get under way there is a natural enthusiasm about their mission which carries them a long way forward with splendid vigor. They make progress in spite of all obstacles; and difficulties that later might become all but fatal to effective service are valiantly overridden.

But all this becomes decreasingly true as organizations increase in size, in age, and in prestige. Hardening of the arteries is a danger of the middle years which can only be withstood as organization leaders give special thought to the problems which age brings. Overcentralized authority, confused responsibilities, a sense of vested rights in jobs, lessened clarity and earnestness about the central aim, the burden of a heavy overhead, the utilization of elaborate plant equipment, the dwindling interest of financial supporters—all these and many other complexities grow up to bedevil the executives of organizations and to create genuine problems of policy, structure, and method which no amount of sheer good will and moral fervor can of themselves solve.

It is, of course, not a matter for individual blame that affairs take this course. It might almost be characterized as a diagnosis of the natural history of human organizations. But the time does nevertheless come when those responsible for the management of associations and institutions have a sense that the whole organism needs to be examined with fresh eyes with a view to prescribing for a combination of ills which together call for treatment effective enough to cure the patient.

That is the excuse for this diagnosis of social, philanthropic, and community agencies which feel that they face problems of internal operation and of relations with the community which in their totality are new in degree if not in kind.

My central theme is that in organizations with aims which get their effect in the minds and hearts of individual members and in their consequent more enlightened and socially effective conduct in the community, *the way the association or institution is set up, controlled, and administered influences directly the possibility of successfully realizing the aims.* Organization structure is a limiting factor upon organized operation. To profess aims of personality growth, of spiritual enrichment, of mental enlargement, and then to carry on with an administrative machinery which is essentially controlled in all essential factors of policy and program from a small, self-perpetuating group at the top, is not merely a confusion of means and ends. It is a basic contradiction in terms which tends to weaken the whole activity of the society.

I shall try to show why this is so and what can be done about it, both in terms of structure and methods of shared participation in policy-making. And I shall try to show that this new way of looking at the task of administration as improved by exercising collective responsibility carries with it a new way of looking at the role of the general executive head—in his relations with his board, with his entire staff, with his committee operations, and with his program formulation and community relations.

The intention is not to offer a manual for the guidance of head administrators so much as it is to present a view of administration as a whole which will help every group in an organization better to understand its role and better to integrate its outlook and efforts with those of everyone else.

I believe also that in our own day, with its economic stresses and differences of opinion and outlook about issues of social readjustment, it is relevant to my main theme to offer, finally, a few suggestions to all the staff members of these organizations as to

8

their individual, personal responsibilities and relations to the community, as these are affected by this new way of looking at organized aims and administrative machinery.

Defining the Organized Aims

I have said that aims should dictate something as to the kind of administrative control and machinery which is used. Why is this so? The answer lies in part in a careful examination of the nature of the aims of the kinds of organization here being considered. I am thinking of associations and institutions organized for religious, civic, social work, educational, character-building purposes—agencies which by various programs are trying to help people to know, to be, and to do *better* whatever will advance their health, happiness, and righteousness in the inevitable community setting of all efforts toward these aspirations.

Such organizations aim at a change in the mind and heart of people, a finer and deeper grasp of life's best values, and a mobilization of energy and passion to help people realize these values. They seek a quickening of intelligence, insight, and emotion which will yield more effective good will among men, a finer and more loyal morale in cooperative efforts to support and create fraternal regard in the world. They seek to point individuals to a way of life for themselves which is at once on a firm foundation of rational reflection, faith, and hope, and which flowers largely in the kind of dealings and relations they have with their fellow men. They are striving, if the phrase is broadly conceived, to help to realize *a rule of good* in the lives of men and women. The ancient injunction to seek first the Kingdom of God has been one of the not unfamiliar idioms in which large sections of society have for generations epitomized the institutional aims I am here recalling to mind only in order to consider their bearing upon acceptable kinds of administrative structure, machinery, and leadership.

Where organizations, for example, seek the realizing of "Christian fellowship," this certainly implies that their own internal affairs should be ordered and operated so that *the process of operation would always and at all points tangibly express fellowship.* A loving attitude toward one's fellow men; the effort to do justice, love mercy, and walk humbly; the intent to act toward others as we would have them act toward us; the active loving of our neighbors as we love ourselves—these are not accidental achievements or by-products of institutional operation. These are, or should be, of the very warp and woof of the hour-by-hour human relations in associations, both among the groups internally related and in the contact of all with the outside world. Obviously, it would seem, they imply something about the kind of organization structure which is set up to advance these aims, about its controls and supervisory methods. Indeed, the very idea of "efficiency" as applied to groups with educational or spiritual aims has to be thoroughly re-examined in relation to those aims. This is said not to cast suspicion on "businesslike" methods, on budgets, or on operating economies. Rather, it emphasizes that we should measure the workings of associated bodies by their success in realizing the basic aim for which they exist.

The fact is, of course, that the democratic ideal, as signifying an assurance of the equal claims of all men to human rights as sons of God, was religiously inspired. Democratic methods and forms were also first experimented with under religious auspices, as a logical institutional expression of the religious affirmation of the worth of human personality. And those experiments in democratic method are still going on in various kinds of organizations, even though many problems remain to be solved.

But one thing seems clear: in organizations where the major concern centers about the development of personality (and all related aims) it is essential that *the democratic idea of organization control be acknowledged* and that honest sustained effort be made to apply it in administering the agency's affairs.

Indeed, the use of ingenuity and educational astuteness in making this application is one of the most fascinating constructive challenges today presented to modern administrators. Here we are on the frontier of new territory in managerial thinking. And if it be objected that such application is impossible, I can only reply that *we have not yet tried out the idea* in any consistent and intelligent way except in scattered instances. In fact, the reason why the very ideas of "organization," of "administration," and of "management" are today receiving fresh examination is because of wide recognition that thus far we have not thought profoundly enough about them to get results which have proved satisfactory in practice.

It is in the light of these profound aims that we have to look at the realities of organized relations as we find them today. With no desire to exaggerate the picture, I nevertheless urge that an examination of present conditions gives rise to misgivings. Typically in the institutions we are here concerned with, there is a board of trustees or directors chosen for various reasons from the "responsible" groups in the community. Some are selected because of their own financial strength or their connection with possible donors; some are chosen for reasons of prestige; some are competent in matters of budget and building operation; and some are representatives of responsible groups of members. We are likely to find local bankers, merchants, chamber of commerce executives, or the wives of these influential members of the community, in positions of power on boards.

And because this is so, the relation of the board to professional staff workers and to all the lesser employees tends all too often to be one essentially of the same master-and-servant character which prevails in business organizations. And the relation of the board to the members or clientele may tend to be tinged with that subtle patronizing quality which is all too likely to arise when one group is trying to "do good to" some other group in the community.

All of this is so usual and so customary that it has tended until recently to be taken for granted by all concerned. Today, however, we do find some questionings about the way in which boards are chosen and the relation to them of the staff and the members. There are instances of "rank-and-file" protest groups, "youth movements" within organizations, efforts to broaden the basis of representation on the controlling body of the association.

There is, in short, a growing feeling abroad that somehow there has to be a wider base for exercising the responsibility for shared activities, that the master-and-servant relation has to be elevated to one of more genuine partnership, that instead of "being done good to" people would prefer to be good and become better in a setting of reciprocal and mutual fellowship.

How can this change in emphasis be brought about?

How can a growing democratic impulse and a growing interest in having personality develop, by giving it a chance for self-choice and self-growth in responsibility and in action, be embodied in the way the individual organization manages its affairs?

In order to answer these questions we have next to examine just what groups typically compose the kinds of institutions we are studying.

Special Group Interests in Organizations

As organizations increase in size it is inevitable that those associated with them come to have different functions and responsibilities and, as this differentiation becomes more marked, the outlooks and interests of these several subgroups tend to become more pronounced and more specialized. If the central aim and unity of drive are to be preserved there has, therefore, to be attention paid to achieving unity in the light of these diverging group points of view; for such unity of drive and intention is the end which must be sought. If the organization is to succeed in fulfilling its aims, special individual or group points of view and interests have to be subordinated to or harmonized with those of the whole body as such. Individuals have to find satisfaction and fulfillment in making the organized aim their own aim. They have to feel a genuine stake in the outcome, as affecting them. Such unity, such harmonizing, are not impossible. But neither are they spontaneous. They have to be striven for. Indeed, this is one of the major tasks of the executive leader.

What subgroups, then, are we likely to find in our associations and institutions?

First, there is the *membership or clientele* itself. They do not necessarily stand first in point of time, for they are usually recruited after the organization opens its doors. But they do exist first in point of importance, since it is for them that the organization exists at all. The college exists for the student; the hospital for the sick; the charity society for the needy; the character-building agency for those whose characters it would help to mold. The danger, of course, always is that the administrators will tend to think almost unconsciously that the organization exists because it is a good thing that it shall exist!

Second, there is the *board of directors or trustees.*

Third, there is the *managerial and professional staff,* including both those who are paid and those who volunteer.

Fourth, there is the *clerical and maintenance staff,* including all office workers, janitors, housekeepers, engineers, restaurant workers, etc.

And, finally, although it is not an integral group within the organization, there should be mentioned the *local community* in which the society does its work. Since the membership and often most of the financial support comes from the locality, the relations which the society has to it and to its special interests cannot be ignored in any effort to understand the interrelationships which have to be provided for and coordinated.

In general, these several participating groups are constituted of different people, often coming from various social and economic levels in the community, usually coming from different age groups, and sometimes from different sexes. And each individual's view of the organization is normally affected by two major influences: first, his attitude as determined by what he does in the organization; second, his view as colored by his total individual, social, and economic outlook, including his interpretation of the agency's purpose.

It cannot be too often said that our work—the attitudes built out of our vocational preoccupations and interest—tend largely to determine our personal view of the problems of groups with which we are associated. A banker on a board of directors tends to think of an organization in terms of budgets and balance sheets. A physical director tends to center his attention on matters of health. A dramatic club director thinks primarily that "the play's the thing."

And not only is this vocational coloring of all our thinking a fact, but we tend naturally and normally to think of ourselves in our institutional connections from the point of view of the satisfactions and benefits which we may personally seek and expect. There is no reason why this should not be so. But to acknowledge it is to realize that, because of the different occupational and personal factors and interests in any organization, there has to be a conscious, explicit effort to transcend special interests in favor of organization unity.

In relation to the several groups just identified, it is useful, therefore, to be candid and realistic as to just what these divergencies of outlook may be in order to see precisely what threats to unity they may bring.

The members or clientele are expecting to realize certain satisfactions and benefits. It is sometimes a nice problem to be sure that they have not been led to expect benefits which are really quite secondary in the aims of the institution; hence it can by no means be taken for granted that they know that they want what the organization may want for them. A swimming pool or a winning football team, for example, may bring in members. But that they bring in members whose aims are in harmony with the association's may not safely be assumed.

The board of directors as the ultimate administrative body is (or should be) concerned to define and give effect to the major aim, and to see that the reputation of the organization in the local community is effectively maintained. Practically, it may become preoccupied with the provision of the sinews of war—with money-raising, balancing budgets, custody of real estate, and the like. The members, or in some cases the members' husbands, are often closely associated with business affairs; and their point of view is likely to be determined by business standards of sound practice, of success, and of administrative methods.

The managerial and professional staff are anxious to be sure that a good professional job is done with reference to more or less definite ideals and standards of good practice. But beyond that they have a natural self-interest to be concerned about the *sufficiency* of their incomes, the *security* of their tenure of employment, and their *status* at work in point of recognition, commendation, and advancement.

More particularly of the head executive himself it may be said that he tends often to identify himself and his interests with those of the board, rather than with those of his staff colleagues. His relations with the leaders of the board are likely to be so close and often of such long standing that he has become mentally one of them; and he thinks of all the rest of the employed group as responsible to the board through him.

The office and housekeeping staffs have perhaps (though not necessarily) a somewhat lesser sense of professional pride. But they, too, have a definite and active concern for sufficiency, security, and status at their own level and to their own degree.

The local community, including donors and well-wishers, expect that the purpose avowed will be served efficiently and economically. They expect "good to be done"—although they are largely dependent upon the leaders of the organization itself to interpret to them what that "good" is and how it is being realized.

15

The disparity of views which the foregoing analysis reveals (however much it may be kept below the surface of conscious acknowledgment) creates a problem for the organization which cannot be ignored or be fobbed off by bland assertions that "of course everyone wants to do the right thing by the organization." It is what *is* the right thing that requires closer scrutiny. And the general line of attack upon this real problem must seemingly be that what is "right" for its several constituent groups has to be brought into open, explicit harmony with what is "right" for the organization.

Basic in thinking about organizations is the assumption or conclusion (from ample evidence) that they are no stronger or more effective in fulfilling their purpose than is the morale of all members and elements. Morale is the mobilization of enthusiasm, intelligence, and energy on behalf of the organized end or goal. Morale is indispensable to sustained creative achievement. It is more than assent or consent. It is zealous devotion. It is the reconciling and unifying of lesser interests and individual loyalties into a *unified* common interest or group loyalty.

How is morale achieved? Certainly not by denying the urgency of the several constituent group and individual points of view and interests. Rather it is by taking account of them, by satisfying them within reason within the frame and effort of the organization's activities. And this integration, where it occurs, is neither inevitable nor accidental. It is a deliberate product of two factors: of *structural* arrangements and of *personal* elements of effective, interpretative leadership. What these two factors mean in this connection and how they may be given effect will presently be suggested.

But it may be well to remind ourselves first that we are not proceeding on any assumption that any particular organization is necessarily good in itself, or that institutions have special and unique interests and concerns which validly stand apart independent of the common interests which those associated with it have agreed they wished to share and forward. Our concern is not to advance every organization at all costs, but rather to be sure that in advancing organizations of agreed vitality, all the means to that advancement shall definitely serve all the associated individuals and their common aim. In fact, in some special cases the concern may be to discover how a given organization, carrying on with a confused or tepid or outgrown aim, can confront itself so candidly as to see whether its aim has lost its validity or whether it can usefully be restated and revitalized.

PRINCIPLES OF CREATIVE COORDINATION

This dilemma of organizations with their aims and individuals with *their* aims can be reconciled. *But we do need to have the tested methods for achieving this constantly before us—both in organizing to act and in leading and supervising the activities and the actors.* There is experience in the history of human institutions which supplies us with the clue to the answer. Out of his study of political life, for example, John Stuart Mill, in his classic *Essay on Representative Government,* reminds us that "the rights and interests of each or any person are only secure from being disregarded when the person interested is himself able and habitually disposed to stand up for them." And he says also that "a people may be unprepared for good institutions; but to kindle a desire for them is a necessary part of the preparation."

Two related principles are based on these truths which throw considerable light on the methods that will integrate group and individual aims:

1. *The principle of the representation of interests,* which says that every special group's interest is safeguarded only as there is an explicit voicing of that interest in the councils of the organization by a representative chosen by and from that group, when issues which affect it are under consideration.

2. *The principle of coordination,* which changes the emphasis from the special groups to the organization and says that the organization functions smoothly only as there is this conscious,

coordinative process of advance agreement throughout the organization upon the general policies and methods which will give its aims effect; and says that this process requires explicit organized group or functional representation in deliberations upon policies which determine outcomes affecting that group.

It is unwise to be more specific as to what will constitute a special "group or functional interest" in any particular organization, since this has to be defined in relation to the elaborateness of the size and structure of that organization, and also in relation to whether the problem under consideration concerns the whole organization or is primarily departmental.

These principles will find equally fruitful application either (1) up and down in a whole organization's vertical line of authority; or (2) within one department; or (3) horizontally among a number of correlated departments which are seeking to integrate their activities. But in respect to whole organizations, some such identification of special interests as the several mentioned above probably achieves an approximation of accuracy where representation and coordination are being sought.

STRUCTURAL AIDS TO COORDINATION

By way of suggesting in more particular terms what these principles may imply in action, I submit a number of propositions which seem at once a sound basis for organization and a sound solution of the dilemma of reconciling institutional and individual objectives:

1. The group in which ultimate authority and responsibility are vested (e.g., the board of directors) should be explicitly composed of representatives of the several major sub-groups which are found to have distinctive outlooks and desires.

2. If the board of directors is thus constituted, it then safely becomes the defensible and logical place where objectives should be established and major policies adopted.

3. The subgroups to be explicitly represented should be so consciously

18

organized as groups that they can select delegates and have their representatives effectively represent them both in initiation of changes and in interpretation of decisions reached.

4. Agenda of board meetings should go to its members long enough in advance to allow a representative reflection of opinion to be secured and brought to the meetings. Also, important new proposals of the board should go back through subgroup representatives for a sounding out of the opinion of constituents.

5. When the board is thus constituted, the general secretary (or whatever title is given to the head executive agent of the board) should be responsible in a major and unified way for the execution of decisions of the board.

6. The number of people reporting directly to this head executive should be limited to the number with whom he or she can have continuous effective contacts as an executive supervisor and leader. When this number is more than ten the danger of inadequate supervision creeps in. The fact that the head executive can and should have useful personal contacts with a far larger number of individuals than this should not be confused with this necessary simplifying of his direct supervisory responsibility.

7. Where there is a "national council" of the organization as a whole with which the local body is affiliated, the line of the adoption and utilization of policies nationally recommended should be only through action of the local board.

These several propositions merit serious consideration with a view to direct, even if gradual, application by organizations and institutions, for the following reasons:

1. A board thus constituted is representative and democratic in a vital sense. It brings it about that all the special interests which have to be reckoned with in reconciling the aim of the whole with the aims of its parts are being currently taken account of. Real integration of aim, policy, and method can thus take place—if there is proper leadership.

2. The aim of the organization can be kept more constantly and clearly in view when all groups participate in considering what the aim is and how it is to be given effect. The danger of institu-

tionalism, of organization for organization's sake, is thus greatly minimized. And positively the sense of responsibility of each member and group for the forwarding of the aim of the organization *as a whole* is thus assured as in no other possible way.

3. The aim of fellowship, with its implications of equal consideration of all members and all related groups, is thus translated into administrative structure and method.

4. The controlling attitudes, policies, and methods of the whole organization are thus *at the outset and continuously* considered, adopted, interpreted, and transmitted in a way best calculated to assure the advance agreement and eager cooperation of all concerned.

5. Everyone in the organization is thus brought to feel a positive and creative stake in the success of the organization. This is true because each has a stake in the initiation and clarification of aims, in the determination of policies relating to sufficiency, security, and status—in short, in seeing to it that organized ends and individual aspirations become harmonized into a cooperative whole.

Another way of putting the reasons why these two principles can be applied so beneficially is supplied in Miss M. P. Follett's phrasing of the case for conscious attention to the coordinative process. She has suggested that the success of this process is assured because:

    a. It achieves a reciprocal relating of all the factors in a situation.
    b. It achieves direct contact of the responsible people concerned.
    c. It achieves all this in the early stages of common deliberation.
    d. It becomes thus, as it should be, a continuing process.*

Several objections will, of course, be made to the general position reflected in these propositions. It will be said that the

---

*See Metcalf, Henry C., and Urwick, L., *Dynamic Administration—The Collected Papers of Mary Parker Follett,* (New York, Harper and Brothers, 1942), p. 297. This entire volume will repay careful study as supporting the point of view of the present volume.

professional, office, and housekeeping staffs are merely the employees of the board; that the members or clientele often do not know what they want or what is for their own best good; that the board does not need or would resent the interference of other groups in major decisions; that this whole process is too circuitous, cumbersome, and slow where important issues have to be decided; that it conduces to an attitude of "bargaining" between the organization and one or more of its component groups.

An honest rereading of these familiar objections will suggest, I submit, to any fair-minded person that they all arise out of a false assumption. These objections assume that certain people are charged to "do good" to others in ways they may safely determine will be good for those others. They assume that in associations created for subjective ends of growth, development, personality enrichment, truth-seeking, these ends can be achieved without active measures and means for giving responsibility, for requiring choices, for fostering consideration of ends and means—*among those who are being guided* no less than among those who guide.

This process of influencing or educating or developing others is in reality a *two-way process*. The benefactor and the benefited are both changed by the process; so too are the teacher and the student, the leader and the follower, the director and the directed. This is not just rhetoric; it is an accurate appraisal of what happens when two groups enter into any close human relations. And if this is literally true, it should be made true also in the definitely *organized* relations encouraged and provided to give a framework to the human relationships which actually exist.

The objections usually faced here arise in part, also, out of a reluctance to admit that human conflicts and disparities of interest are a fact in associated efforts. Many people animated by good will forget that conflict has its constructive and creative role. Yet if an organization as a whole is not strong, clear, and confident enough about what it wants to do to be able to compose the kinds of internal differences which I have suggested as actually present and as always potentially likely to become more articulate,

21

then one of two things is wrong. Either what the organization wants to do is not clearly seen by all as being worthy of everyone's effort to "get on the band wagon." Or, to put it more positively, the leadership in the organization is not sufficiently effective to summon all to an individually satisfying loyalty which rises above lesser differences.

We have, then, up to this point considered the organized aims and presumably found them good. Let us now take a look at the part to be played by leadership in creating unity.

Leadership as an Aid to Coordination

I have already said that organization morale and unified operation depend: (1) upon a structure and machinery which aid coordination; and (2) upon the right quality of personal leadership to facilitate the coordinating. (*See page 16*)

Turn now to the contribution which leadership peculiarly must make. It should, in a word, galvanize the whole process of conferring and integrating diverse interests into a smooth-running experience of human relations among the individuals and groups whose efforts are being unified.

This means and implies a number of supporting factors. It means that the leader is constantly holding the main, common objective in view, so that in deliberative conferences on policy and methods someone is always bringing discussion back to the main track and toward the anticipated terminal point of agreement.

He it is also who will be specially concerned in the various groups where he is overseeing the coordinative process to see that the following conditions are satisfied: (1) a complete body of facts available about matters at issue; (2) an open consideration of every different point of view before any given deliberative body; (3) the encouraging of subordination of differences in favor of unity of drive; (4) the effort to assure that indecision changes into choice and action; (5) provision for the process of acquainting the entire membership with decisions and of interpreting them persuasively; (6) the careful delegating of responsibility for carrying out decisions.*

Experience is conclusive that unless the leader assumes these responsibilities, they are not fulfilled and the process of coordination halts and breaks down. And in such organizations as those here discussed, the general secretary is the logical executive to undertake this leading role. He it is who definitely should take the *whole* view of the whole organization. He it is who should have a sufficiently sympathetic and comprehensive view of the entire operation to facilitate the bringing together of different outlooks.

Also, more than this is required, even to aid coordination. There must be continuously sympathetic account being taken and consideration being given to points of view and claims advanced by sincere minority groups which want to be unified with the whole but feel that they have some special insight or emphasis of which adequate account is not being taken. And this consideration must go beyond the usual efforts to integrate differences which are always arising about minor points. It has to do, where profound issues are raised or joined, with the general executive's own insight and prophetic vision of the larger trend that affairs are taking as they relate to the protests of these minorities. I am, in short, not implying that a facile smoothing over of differences or a mollifying of minorities is the road for the executive to follow. On occasion his line of policy may be so under fire that the effort to coordinate may have to be preceded by his own searching of soul as to the implications of the issue which the minority has raised.

In order, next, to be more specific about how the general executive works with the various groups which have to be brought into working unity, a few suggestions will be offered about his relations: first with the board; next with the professional staff and the balance of paid employees; and finally with committees in general.

---

* For further elaboration of all this, see my book, *The Art of Leadership,* Chap. VII.

The board of directors or trustees, especially as at present constituted and therefore often not too closely related to the day-by-day functioning of the organization, inevitably creates certain problems for the general executive which can be solved only by paying special heed to them. In the first place, the relation of this executive to the board may need clarification. Is he or she the "hired man" or agent of the board? Or is the definitive leadership vested in this individual with the board acting in the background as guide and counselor? If the board does hire the general executive (which would be usual), does this jeopardize his basic effectiveness as leader?

It seems clear that the general executive should ideally have sufficient capacity and personality to rise above the fact that he is technically in the employ of the board and responsible legally to it; and for all practical purposes he should assume the acknowledged leadership. This will be sound, not because this executive should dominate the board or assume that he has a vested right in his position, but because both from the standpoint of new vision and planning, and also from the point of view of clearly centralized operating responsibility, *there has to be a head.*

And if the general secretary is to be this head with the greatest effectiveness, it is probably desirable that he should enter into a contract with the board for specified periods. This would give him reasonable independence during incumbency while giving the board periodic opportunity to renew the contract or not. Obviously, of course, the whole relationship should always rise above the level of contract to a level of fellowship and harmonious intention. But the fact remains that the method of relating the general executive to the organization should be explicit, should encourage real leading guidance from him, and should get away from any suggestion that he is only the agent or mouthpiece of the board.

The good executive, however, carries weight with his board,

not because he has an iron-clad contract, but because he works with them in ways that get results which both he and they think important. Real leadership on his part, therefore, consists in applying most fully the collective wisdom of the whole board to problems arising as to the creative guidance of the organization. Lofty as this ideal may sound, it calls in a workaday world for the most practical application on the part of the executive of foresight, tact, and persuasiveness. If even a good board is to perform at its best, it must continuously feel not only that there are new worlds to conquer, but that it *can* conquer some of them. To the end of strengthening this mood the following hints may be helpful:

1. The general executive should get the board to consider problems when they have become, or threaten to become, troublesome to the board. There is a wise sense of timing to be employed in choosing the psychological moment when a difficulty is imminent, genuine, and pressing. We have always to remember that people think to best advantage *when a problem is disturbing them.* Sometimes the shrewd leader will be able to foresee and anticipate problems so that they can be considered as pressing before they become too crucial. But even this can only be done when the board can be made genuinely concerned by the issue. Sometimes, also, it will be good tactics to let some issue come to a crisis (at least from the board's point of view), in order that the board will be aroused, will deliberate, and will act.

It should be axiomatic that problems will be faced only when all involved recognize them *as* problems. It is the board's and not the executive's awareness of a problem which alone will bring its members to grips with it.

2. The executive should be sure that the board has the same data to work upon in solving a problem as he himself has had. And if he has a solution which he wants the board to reach, he must give the members of the board time to be exposed to the same data and to think through a solution in much the same way that he has done.

3. The executive may bring issues to the point of being felt to be problems by the board, in terms, for example, of: (a) sharp conflicts of attitude and points of view within the organization as a whole (as, for instance, when a radical group wishes to hire the association's meeting hall); (b)

25

financial shortages, threatened losses, or budget difficulties; (c) confusion, vagueness, or opposition on the part of any considerable group of members regarding aims or methods of realizing them; (d) criticisms by outsiders.

4. In dealing with the board, collectively and individually, it is important for the executive to know the kinds of approach which are most effective. Some will see a new project first in terms of its cost; others in terms of the prestige it will bring to the association—or even to themselves; others will consider first the religious values involved or their responsible relationship to "the cause"; still others will feel most deeply their identification with the group of members concerned in the project.

Similarly, the manner of presenting data to individual members most effectively will differ with the mental characteristics of each. Some learn most readily through the ear—through being told in conversation. Some prefer to get information through reading. Some are predominantly motor-minded and acquire ideas best in the arena of action.

5. These observable differences in human reactions suggest the truth that often some of the most effective work with board members will be done *with individuals between meetings* no less than at meetings. The good executive leader will constantly keep himself on such a personal and social footing with his board members that this type of contact and interchange can be of a friendly and informal character.

6. The general executive will be persuasive also to the extent that he is clear as to *what* he wants in major matters; knows *why* he wants it; and is reasonably clear as to *how* in definite terms it can be obtained. This does not imply that he tries to override others, but rather that his sense of direction is clear while he tries to be effective in persuasion.

7. A further tactic in his persuasiveness will be a discreet use of the reenforcement of his own views by calling in those who for any reason will have weight with the board. This may, for example, mean using members of a "national council," representatives of similar organizations from other localities, public notables, or experts in special fields.

8. The general executive should also be at pains to keep the work of the organization "sold" to his board in terms of concrete achievement. This argues that he should study, to be sure he uses methods of reporting and adopts measures of progress which will be at once as definite, objective, and persuasive as possible, both to his board and to donors in general.

In organizations with subjective aims this task presents real difficulties. And one danger that the entire administrative group of an organization may have to fight is the temptation to apply quantitative measures to qualitative facts. In an organization like the Y.M.C.A. or the Y.W.C.A., for example, the interpretation to the boards, as at present constituted, of youth itself and of its aspirations, its problems, and its vocabulary, may well be a major assignment of the general executive. (If the board is constituted as recommended early in this study, this kind of interpretation will tend to take place spontaneously and in the natural course of events within the board itself.)

9. In line with the assignment suggested above, the executive should aim to make all board meetings educational processes in the best sense. This means that however much decision *making* may seem to be the major role of the board, the process of decision *reaching* should be patiently (though tactfully) kept prominently in mind by the executive leader.

10. Real issues of policy will arise with boards. It may even be true that they are destined to arise more acutely in the future than in the past. Where such differences seem for the time being too serious to reconcile, it may be good tactics for the executive to ask the board, when its members are doubtful about a new proposal, *to allow it to be tried for an experimental period* of agreed length, after which results will be reviewed and a reconsideration of the policy take place. It was a wise philosopher who observed that many a horse which did not know it was thirsty, when led to water found that it liked to drink!

When an issue becomes really acute, the executive may even feel impelled finally to say, "What you ask me to do runs counter to my judgment and to my conscience. You certainly wouldn't want me to act contrary to my own deep conviction in this matter?" Usually the answer to this question would be a renewed effort to integrate conflicting views. But if the board at such a point and on an issue felt to be fundamental by the executive demands that he take a line of action opposed to his conviction, there may be but one course to be honorably followed: to ask the board to allow him to resign from fulfilling the remainder of his contract.

Undoubtedly a little more courage and independence in times

27

of crisis would strengthen the professional standing of staff members, rather than the opposite.

It may be objected that the foregoing counsels imply too great an attempt at manipulation of people on the part of the executive. But all that has been said above only brings into the open what is more or less the working method of the successful leader anyway. Manipulation in a certain sense occurs inevitably where leaders are trying to get things done. The only serious question is as to whether what the leader is trying to do is truly valuable; and if it is, he is not only within his rights but he is merely being intelligent if he studies the methods of personal influence which do in fact prove effective.

Moreover, in all honesty it should be acknowledged that others with whom the executive is working closely are probably studying him with some care (and should!) to discover "how his mind works," and what lines of approach will find him responsive. Here again we should admit the inevitable existence of a two-way process in which the odds are by no means always in favor of the executive!

Again it may be objected that the suggestions above imply a slighting regard for the value of the board to the organization. Nothing is farther from my intention than this. It has to be recognized that the people who give generously or supervise the expenditure of resources which others have given are naturally concerned to be sure that money is wisely spent. More than that, it is a wise check upon the organization that this should be so. The keeper of the common purse should certainly disperse funds only on the assurance that the outlay is justifiable. This is quite a different thing, however, from letting him who pays the piper call the tune!

Indeed, instead of minimizing the board's importance, which may be a real danger, I venture to suggest that its members should be *more* used, especially where they are able to make contributions (not financial) which can be wrought into the active day-by-day work of the agency. General secretaries could in many cases draft much superior ability for direct service if they were to devote more attention to this possibility. There is unquestionably an educational service to be rendered in this direction from which everyone would benefit—the membership and staff no less than the volunteer.

THE GENERAL EXECUTIVE AND COMMITTEE WORK

I have alluded to the importance of being sure that whatever committee action takes place makes use of current knowledge about improved ways to carry on conferences. But a few further separate observations are in order with special reference to strengthening the processes of executive coordination.

Two extremes of practice are frequently to be noted here, both of which will lessen the coordinative value of committee work. Either an organization minimizes the value of committees because of the claim that they lead to confused responsibility and delay in action. Or their value is too highly regarded and too much executive responsibility is given them. It is to preserve a proper balance between these two extremes that the following conclusions are offered about the proper limits upon committee functioning in relation to the executive task.

If we recall that executive work involves planning, supervising, coordinating, laying down policies, and the like, it is clear that committees can often forward certain of these processes. A House Committee, a Budget Committee, or a Personnel Committee may correctly have delegated to it a definite mandate in a segment of the executive field.

One major task is to be sure that it does its job. This assurance rests ultimately with the general executive and directly with the chairman of the committee. Or if it is a committee of the board, appointed by its head, this same responsibility would fall upon the chairman of the board.

The committee has become for the purpose in hand the agent

29

of the executive. And if fruitful committee action is to result, the chairman of the committee should be looked upon as the agent of the executive in accomplishing the committee's assignment and as the agent of the committee in dealings with the executive. The chairman is the one the executive has a right to look to for accomplishment.

Several conditions have to be fulfilled:

1. The mandate to the committee from the executive must be clear—as to subject, scope, and authority.

2. The executive should look to the committee chairman for results, and the committee (in the absence of definite assignment to others) should look upon its chairman as its own focal point and executive agent.

3. A time limit should be set for the fulfilling of a committee's mandate.

4. If certain overt actions are to be taken (such as submitting a budget, hiring a housekeeper, directing the alterations or repairs of plant) some *member* of the committee as an individual should be specifically charged with the task. By its nature the committee is fitted to take counsel, reach agreements, adopt policies (the board of directors itself being a case in point). To this extent it is correctly executive. But equally by its nature the committee as such is *not* qualified for activity which requires individualized, clear-cut, active performance of specific duties. The danger of confusion here has always been great. A committee, for example, is charged to draw up a budget. This is a legitimate delegation of a certain executive responsibility. But the work gets done only as the whole task on its operating side is broken down into a group of correlated but individualized duties and *each member is directed to specific tasks* so that his labors comprise a needed part of the whole assignment. To assume that because "a committee is going to do this," it will necessarily be done is, of course, fatuous. A committee does something only as its members each do the right thing. And that depends largely upon the guidance of the chairman.

5. All of this makes the selection of a committee's membership a matter of great importance. Only those should be selected to be members who have a vital contribution to make to the carrying out of its mandate. This implies contributions of knowledge, of points of view, of desires, of skills—as related to the purpose.

6. Committee action is further facilitated by: (a) a careful *recording* of decisions reached; (b) a careful *transmission* of decisions to the proper executive person or group; (c) a careful *timing* of meetings and interim periods to be sure that the elapsed times are reasonable to assure that accomplishment will result.

In a word, committees can be executive, *within the limits set forth above*. They can be responsible, effective, and not unduly dilatory. Indeed, they are an indispensable means for doing certain kinds of things. Fundamentally they are agents of integration—for bringing agreement out of disagreement or confusion. However much they may seem to involve delay and to generate too much talk, they are nevertheless *the price of advance agreement*. And within the given limits, nothing else can take their place. They are a tool of the democratic, knowledge-pooling, and desire-harmonizing process which cannot be otherwise forwarded.

And when committees fail, as they sometimes do, it is because the limits to their role are not clearly understood or because they have not benefited by proper leadership from the chairman.

A special type of committee service which, perhaps, calls for more explicit mention is the advisory committee to a single department, function, or activity. Such a committee would, preferably, be sanctioned and instructed as to its powers, responsibilities, and duties by the board of directors. And its purely advisory role should be clearly stipulated, so that its members, even though they may be in direct personal contact with the department executive with whom they are advising, will keep their actions within necessary limits. A board might, for example, appoint a lay advisory committee to help oversee and confer with the Physical Department and the work of its director. But it should be kept clearly in view that the assistance of such a committee does not alter the fact that the physical director reports to the general secretary in carrying out an established policy, program, and budget. This advisory committee may well have helped to shape the policy, and may wish to recommend changes in it; but its powers should be confined to advising with the general secretary or the board as to the wisdom of having such changes authorized by the secretary. It will be a source of confusion and difficulty if such a committee tries to give direct instructions to the physical director. In short, its powers are limited to advice and persuasion, and without this limitation the whole idea of unity of command is seriously impaired.

THE GENERAL EXECUTIVE AS ADMINISTRATOR

If, as suggested earlier, the general executive should have only a relatively few executives reporting and directly responsible to him, one of his first problems as his institution increases in size is to see to it that a logical and practical division of responsibilities and functions is achieved. For example, it should be possible to place all the housekeeping or maintenance staff under one person qualified by training in institutional management to head up this work. What other duties and functions are sufficiently major to be sensibly grouped together for executive oversight will depend upon the size of the organization and upon the nature and variety of its program and activities.

Irrespective of the size of the organization, however, the general executive should have a clear picture, *preferably in writing,* of all the duties and functions for which someone has to be responsible. To see that all duties are allocated, it is essential from the standpoint of operating efficiency that the general executive knows what he is responsible for and exactly what each of his staff is responsible for. There is good reason to believe that general executives tend to try to carry too great a load, to have their fingers in too many pies, to be responsible for too great a variety of functions. In periods of financial retrenchment this may be inevitable. But it should be a matter for major concern that the top executive have time enough to be sure that *he and his organization are constantly holding to the main objective.*

Upon him rests the special responsibility for adjusting programs, activities, public appeals, and public relations of all kinds to the constantly shifting trends of public interest and of community needs. The basic underlying aim may in a sense seem to remain "the same, yesterday, today and forever." But the translation of that aim into terms understandable by and appealing to each generation requires adaptations of appeal and program. This is equally true in the church, in education, in social work, in charity organization societies, and in associations like the Y.M.C.A. or the Y.W.C.A. The restating of aim with the current sense of need, the dramatizing of purpose in harmony with the felt concerns of each generation—these are perennial problems. And that general executive is avoiding his major task who does not plan to devote definite hours to sober study of these inevitable transitions of emphasis in community interest and need. In this aspect of his work he has always the problem of being sure he is carrying along with him the understanding and cooperative support of his entire professional staff.

What this involves in specific efforts to know at close range the local community, to know the broader trends of social, political, economic, and religious change, to know the new experience of similar bodies in other localities, can only be suggested here.* But these are all responsibilities for the discharge of which the executive *must have free time.* And he should, of course, have the kind of grasp of his task which fires him with zeal to assume these responsibilities continuously throughout his working career. The world does not stand still; and no institution or program is ever once and for all adapted to fulfilling its mission most effectively. New times are always demanding new measures and new men—or men with minds open to new ideas.

The general executive should, then, identify clearly the operating functions his organization has to perform and see to it that some person is assigned to carry out each one. The duties, responsibilities, and authority of each departmental executive should be assigned to him just as definitely as possible and with clear recognition of the amount of work the individual can reasonably do.

---

* See, as an excellent example of method of study here, the check list in the *Woman's Press* (September, 1935), pp. 413-416.

He should in this connection see that distinction is observed between the powers and rights of "line" as against "staff" executives. A housekeeper or a chief engineer is, for example, a line executive. There is a line of operating authority for duties in these areas from (presumably) the head executive, to housekeeper, to cooks, to kitchen helpers, etc. Line executives are those in a hierarchy of responsibility for delivery of service (or product) from top to bottom supervisory positions. Staff executives, on the other hand, do not have this direct kind of responsibility for specific operating results (except with their only immediate departmental assistants). Suppose, for example, you have a public relations executive or a central purchasing agent. Each presumably reports to the head executive and has duties of facilitation which serve the needs of all line departments. But they may not tell line department heads what to do as to operating methods. They are advisers, consultants, and aids helping with specialized assistance, and securing their results by the persuasive rightness of their suggestions rather than by "issuing orders" beyond their own immediate departmental area. It is vital to smooth operation that these two kinds of executive work be kept distinguished in the minds of all. No staff executive as such should be found issuing definite orders to line department heads. And when, on occasion, an individual may serve part-time in a line and part-time in a staff capacity, the need for careful separation of powers is even greater.

The general executive next has the duty of assuring that all the agreed functions are performed. This implies that both by personal contacts and by whatever forms of reports are most explicit, he is supervising the forwarding of activities.

He has also the major responsibility for coordination of all activities into a unified, consistent whole in relation to his vision of objectives and to the agreements which have been reached on policies and methods. This, as has already been said, involves effective use of structures—that is, coordinating agencies such as committees—and the supplying of personal leadership within the coordinating processes themselves.

In order to do all this well, he should have a conscious mastery of performance in the following areas of individual and social psychology:

1. The steps in the problem-solving process (see my *Human Nature and Management*, Chap. VIII, "How to Encourage Reasoning").

2. The steps in the teaching process and its correlate, the learning process (see my *Human Nature and Management*, Chap. VI, "The Learning Process," and Chap. XVI, "The Technique of Training"; and also my *The Art of Leadership*, Chap. VIII, "The Leader as Teacher," and Chap. XVI, "How to Train Leaders").

3. The implications of the "psychology of the evolving situation" (see my *Human Nature and Management*, Chap. II, "The Psychological Point of View"; also my *The Art of Leadership*, pp. 276-282).

4. The technique of conference and committee action (see my *Human Nature and Management*, Chap. XIV, "The Technique of Group Action"; also my *The Art of Leadership*, Chap. X, "The Leader as Conference Chairman").

Since I have elsewhere, as indicated, discussed these four skills in some detail, I take the liberty of referring the reader to those discussions, which are more extended and adequate than space here allows.

A further truth about executive action which underlies this entire study is that there has always to be a parallelism and interdependence between two kinds of effort if organizations are to function properly. There is an inherent complementary duality, for example, between

> good will and good methods
> attitude   and structure
> intention and performance
> motive   and mechanism

And if any of the mental sets suggested in the left-hand column above are ever to be translated out of the realm of wish into that tangible attainment, this can be done only through specific, creative, and planned action. The mental outlook has always to be implemented to be effective, and the quality of the outlook is really no better than that of the overt performance.

The General Executive and His Staff

In relation to all the individuals who are hired to help carry on the work and in relation to volunteers as well, some one or more executives is in fact responsible for the terms and conditions of employment and for the effectiveness with which all these individual efforts are related to the total organization effort. This whole task involves a considerable variety of duties which have now come to be spoken of as the *personnel function* in management. Briefly, its work is usually considered to include selection, training, provision of suitable working conditions, negotiation of proper terms of employment (wages, hours, vacations, etc.), adjustments of individual difficulties, provisions as to accident, old age and illness, and all the more general features which may be found to benefit morale and generate a cooperative spirit.

The detailed ways in which an organization decides to handle the foregoing matters would constitute its *personnel policy.* And obviously every organization, *irrespective of its size,* and whether it realizes it or not, does have this personnel function to carry out and does have a personnel policy controlling its human dealings. It is important that the existence of this function be always clearly acknowledged, however small the group being directed, and that the policy be one which has been conscientiously and thoughtfully arrived at.

There are several ways to assure adequate recognition of this function and explicit adoption of sound policies. Many associations find, for example, that a personnel committee can formalize concern over these matters in the large and guide individual executives in giving sympathetic effect to the personnel policy in its individual applications. But for this personnel committee to work to best effect I suggest that the principle of representation of interests as set forth above should certainly be applied in the selection of its membership. The typical present practice of having personnel policies set essentially by the board and applied through the agency of the general executive seems unduly autocratic and not mindful enough of the structural conditions which will help to build morale, confidence, and unity among the enlisted personnel.

Even if the organization is large enough to warrant the employment of a full-time personnel executive (or have one executive, such as the general secretary, who is responsible for the personnel function on a part-time basis), the value of a representative advisory personnel committee can be great; for it can help to facilitate the whole task of formulating, interpreting, and gaining acceptance for the policies which are to prevail.

Whatever formal provision is made for assigning responsibility for this function, however, it has always to be borne in mind that the personnel policy in many of its details gets its effect with individual workers mainly through the attitude and behavior of their own department heads. And to that extent the personnel policy is actually *no better than the behavior of every supervisor demonstrates it to be.* Every supervisory person has to treat his own group in line with the prevailing policies—or the policies do not prevail. There is a continuing major administrative responsibility here to be sure that all supervisors and departments are in fact translating a good policy in good ways.

One other general observation should be made about the attitude with which the personnel function is approached. Each individual employed or volunteering in the organization is charged with the carrying on of some function—or he should not be there. All are in this sense "functionaries," and all are in this sense equally indispensable to the total effort. There may be "higher" and "lower" in respect to the quality of skill required for a given function; and there may be "more" or "less" in respect to the available supply of certain skills. But there is a genuine *equality* of *need* from the organization's standpoint for everyone who is engaged upon a real function. This equality of need argues something vital as to the equality of consideration which should be accorded to every individual in relating him to the institution.

There is, of course, a sense in which no one individual is indispensable to the organization. It presumably has its momentum of purpose and going effectiveness apart from whether this or that person occupies this or that position. But the necessary positions do have to be filled, and to give full thought to the personal satisfactions of the present incumbent in each post is the condition of resultful cooperation.

It is impossible to be completely specific as to what will constitute a good personnel policy or what will be found to be "fair" terms of employment in any given case. As to the former, a broad set of desirable standards is today generally acknowledged to exist, and these we have set forth in an earlier work.* As to the latter, local circumstances will of course be governing. But that certain classifications of work and ranges of compensation for these can be established has already been repeatedly established.**

There is a grave, if not openly admitted danger, however, that in organizations of the kind here primarily under consideration the boards or the general executive will try almost unconsciously to exploit the loyalty and devotion of the paid staff because they are working "in a good cause." The temptation is great to assume that all others are as devoted as the executive and that they therefore will readily accept terms and conditions of employment which are really inadequate.

This is a real issue which is accentuated by present methods of relatively autocratic administrative setup. This again points to the importance of a reasonably objective set of standards regarding the professional worth of positions relatively within the organization and comparatively with other organizations. Certainly the apologetic or self-depreciating note is to be avoided by

---

* See *Personnel Administration: Its Principles and Practice,* by Ordway Tead and H. C. Metcalf (New York, McGraw-Hill Book Co., 1933).

** See, for example, the excellent pamphlet, *A Personnel Manual,* by Jessamine C. Fenner (New York, The Woman's Press, 1933).

employees in dealing with boards on these matters. Here is not merely a question of balancing budgets. There may be on occasion a deeper question as to whether the board and the community are sufficiently convinced of the value of an organization to be able to compensate its staff well enough for them to serve at all with real efficiency.

All this is not said to belittle the glory of sacrificial work by a devoted staff. But the laborer is worthy of his hire. And beyond a certain trial period, inability to secure support may be due to community obtuseness to its own needs; or it may be due to the fact that the organization has not demonstrated that it serves a vital function.

One thing is clear. In a worldly society, preoccupied with many things, laborers in the vineyard of the mind and spirit should appraise themselves and their work with self-respect and a decent sense of self-worth. Humility has for literal survival to be balanced by a certain self-assurance, by a confident awareness of one's value. This means, for one thing, that the general executive endeavors to meet the members of the board and the donors *as a complete equal.* The fact that his standard of "success" and "getting on" may be different from theirs alters not at all the fact that *he believes that he and his staff have a function in society which is vital and significant.* Unless the employees hold their heads high and are not on the defensive about their tasks, they will not be accorded the consideration they merit.

A still further factor today increasingly complicates the personnel work of our institutions, particularly in relation to the non-professional employees. Under our Federal social security legislation, employees of all sorts of philanthropic and meliorative agencies are at present exempted from the provisions of unemployment compensation and old-age pensions. This means that in the labor market such organizations will stand at a distinct disadvantage in offering jobs to people because of the lesser protection against these risks which they will get. It may well mean a tendency to find the less preferred workers the only ones available for and willing to take positions. To the extent that this proves true, it will be a handicap to good morale. Somehow, it would seem that *equivalent advantages* will have to be offered to employees of all these agencies, or their personnel policies will be competitively unfavorable and the employed personnel will be less satisfactory.

PROGRAMS IN RELATION TO AIMS

Ideally, the activities and program which an organization carries on are the tangible evidence of the ways by which it believes it can realize its avowed aims.

Practically, all programs get crystallized and rigid, and the need for revaluation is perennial. Why is this? One factor in character-building associations, for example, is that sometimes parts of a program are originally developed with the secondary aim of "getting members into the association." Then, when they are in, they will presumably be guided to or exposed to the primary aim. As tactics this is, no doubt, legitimate. But the danger always is that the organization itself and the members on their side will get so immersed in carrying on the secondary efforts that they have not the means nor the time nor even the inclination for the main drive. The means thus become the end.

Another factor making for the outmoding of programs is the changing vocabulary, idiom, and outlook of the oncoming generations. Words are subtle instruments. The danger that they will not mean the same thing to different people and particularly to different age groups is tremendous. Such words, for example, as "democracy," "personality," "self-expression," "self-realization," "character," "leadership," "socialism," "God," "Christianity," are only hints as to the points at which confusion can arise as to what people are talking about when they use them. Also, there are fashions and fads in words, which cannot be ignored when it comes to voicing and articulating the aims of organizations with subjective ends.

40

A third factor is that, because every organization operates in the social setting of a given time and place, the social (or total combined external) influences playing upon that body change from time to time. Today, for example, speaking in general terms, we are seemingly coming out of an age of so-called "individualism"—where the rugged qualities of individualistic assertiveness, of acquisitiveness, of competitive zeal for personal advancement, were wrought into the outlook of the generation. The emphasis increasingly seems now to be upon efforts in all areas of living which are associated, cooperative, organizational, and collective in the broadest sense.

Unquestionably the character qualities now favored differ markedly from those favored in the nineteenth century. Do programs and policies take sufficient account of this?

A fourth factor derived from the third is that economic forces may so alter the status and relations of different groups in the community that the question, "Whom are we ministering to?" may present a vexing problem. Certain organizations may perhaps reasonably claim to be largely serving people who come from the middle class. Here again we are confronted with another ambiguous wording. Who composes this group, and what are its aspirations, needs, and problems? Here is seemingly an urgent problem to at least some of those organizations being discussed—a problem closely related to the evaluation of their programs. It is not inconceivable that the whole relation of this "middle class" to the rest of society in America, in respect to its political interests, its social demands, and its economic insecurities, is today in such fundamental transition that any organization which is in fact serving a middle class clientele can hardly avoid bewilderment within its own ranks as to the objectives it holds, their validity and interpretation.

A final factor, again related in part to vocabulary but related also to attitude, is the lessening interest and belief in the idea of "doing good to others," as that has been popularly interpreted. In a profound way and in the long look, people in a democracy somehow feel that they do not want "to be done good to." There is to the sensitive spirit a world of difference between the attitude which says, "Love thy neighbor as thyself," and that which says, "My ideal is to do good to others." The one is a high, disinterested conception of a consciousness of a reciprocal relation of mutual value among individuals in society. The other tends to be a self-centered interest in using the influence one can exert upon others as the means for one's own "salvation." The one recognizes that most people do in fact make a contribution to well-being through their normal pursuits, and could undoubtedly make a far greater contribution if the neighborly aim were consciously and intelligently striven for. The other, especially if carried to a logical extreme, means that always in conduct someone must be the benefactor and someone else the beneficiary, and that the beneficiary may be hard-pressed to find out how he in his turn may be the benefactor. The one is spiritually democratic; the other spiritually aristocratic or snobbish—and it may even be priggish.

The fact is that people do not want to "be served." They may want to be taught and guided and inspired. The sound relationship (with its resultant attitudes) in contemporary society is one of mutuality, of reciprocal creativeness, of common striving for ends jointly arrived at and cooperatively held. It implies and looks for a transfer of the attitude of neighborliness and friendly concern from one to another in wider and wider spheres of influence. The seer and the prophet will always do us the great service of supplying the vision which leads us on over the next hill. But the acceptance of that vision is an individual act of voluntary self-enlistment for those who can be helped to see the light and "follow in his train."

It should be pointed out, therefore, that the use of the word "fellowship," for example, in voicing the objectives of both the Y.M.C.A. and the Y.W.C.A. is a splendid recognition of the difference of emphasis and attitude that I am trying to express as between yesterday and today. The problem now becomes one of translating and dramatizing that fellowship conception into both structures and program contents in order that they may in fact encourage the growth of human associations animated by this democratic attitude and this sense of spiritual equality.

If it be objected that all of these factors do not in reality have much bearing upon the aims and programs of organizations, I can only answer that the testimony which comes to me from within the ranks of the organizations themselves is somewhat disconcerting. The questions are often heard: "What *do* we stand for today? How shall we appeal to the new generation? Is our organization performing the function it should?"

And if this kind of corrosive doubt exists in any widespread way, there is but one thing to do. *The organization must re-examine its objectives and its program content.* Is it doing *in today's terms* the essential thing it originally set out to do? Is it at work upon its own "big idea"? It is only after these questions are faced and answered that the program problem can be constructively attacked.

But when they are answered, I believe a second conclusion may perhaps then be reached, namely, that the content of the program is less important than its *intent*. It is not so much what is being done as it is *how that contributes to the major aim* which has to be considered. A rooming house can be run "to the glory of God," or it can just be one more inexpensive place in which young people can live decently. Of course there are more and less effective forms of activity. A discriminating sense as to which activities have presumably greater educational value will give much guidance here. But the idea, for example, that certain parts of a program are "religious" and certain other parts are secular, is pernicious. Either the whole program all the time is shot through with a sense of worthfulness, worthiness, wholeness, and holiness; or it is not. And the effort has, of course, to be to infuse a clear sense of the main drive into *every* action and effort of the organization, whether it be running a basketball game, renting rooms, or directing a janitor.

43

Is this particular activity counting definitely and heavily in carrying us on toward our goal?

That is the question which boards of trustees and head executives must unflinchingly ask themselves about the entire program at not too infrequent intervals.

And it is not impossible that executives will occasionally find under this persistent questioning that they are carrying along a rather heavy freight of out-dated, superfluous, or ineffective activities, which if thrown out the window would give the organization more time and resources for activities nearer to the core of the task it originally set itself to do.

BUILDING THE PROGRAM

I have throughout this study been suggesting, at least by implication, that many of the problems faced by meliorative organizations today are new, in form if not in substance. Or, if they are not new, they are certainly urgent and pressing for attention with new insistence.

If I may attempt to locate the heart of the difficulty faced, the problem is how to make the appeal of the good life persuasive and controlling in the life of the oncoming generation in the face of the uncertainties, confusions, insecurities, conflicts, and fears which the total social situation of our day presents. This is a difficulty which has dual aspects: that of individual adjustment and that of the conditions and limiting influences of the environment. To put it another way, each individual is the product of personal drives and capacities, and a product no less of the whole intellectual, economic, and spiritual climate of his time. Economic determinism is not the whole story, nor yet is "free will" the whole story. The meaning and conditions of "freedom" have to be discovered; the modifying part played by economic and related factors has to be understood.

And perhaps this latter field is at the moment in need of the greater attention and greater clarification on the part of those who manage institutions and social agencies—not because it is necessarily more important absolutely, but because in relation to our day and hour it is the factor with which we have all shown ourselves least able to come effectively to grips. Or at least it is in relation to our comprehension of this part of the problem that we need to think through again the total problem of the supporting and environmental ways and means, no less than the subjective dynamics, of the good life.

What, then, can organizations with mental and spiritual aims *do* in this direction?

I do not propose to elaborate details of method, but rather to suggest in outline the mandate which the nature of today's difficulties seems to impose upon us. Details must in any event be adapted to particular local needs and conditions.

The need for *knowledge and comprehension of our times* seems to me the first requirement. Of the necessary action based on this understanding I shall speak presently. And this need for understanding seems to exist among boards, staffs, and members or clientele. Some specific suggestions as to ways of getting knowledge might, for example, be as follows:*

1. Encourage groups within the organization (boards, staff, clubs, etc.) to undertake systematic study and discussion of the meaning of current affairs, political, economic, and social. This may well include the creation of *ad hoc* committees and conferences to examine into special questions (e. g., child labor, minimum wage, neutrality, etc.). It may well include also the more active interest of such groups in following specifically the legislative activities of local boards of aldermen, state legislatures, and the national Congress.

2. Encourage special groups to undertake surveys of special problems in the local community (e. g., public utility rates, housing, cost of living). If the results of such surveys prove more valuable as education for the researchers than as a basis for publication, that does not necessarily lessen the value of these efforts.

---

* I am indebted to Mr. J. E. Sproul for suggestions here, growing out of committee deliberations of an institute of Y.M.C.A. secretaries held at Silver Bay.

3. Encourage such groups as those mentioned in 1 and 2 to make trips of inspection and study to see local conditions, institutions, and activities.

4. Help local groups to come together to discover and consider their common outlooks, interests, and problems (e. g., consumers in general or of particular products or services, office workers, members of some industrial group).

5. Encourage the conduct of forums or panels to discuss timely problems under enlightened direction and guidance.

6. Help other local organizations (Chambers of Commerce, Rotary Clubs, Men's Clubs, etc.) to select topics and secure speakers who will be truly informative on various sides of current issues.

7. Help groups of unemployed to cooperate in retraining vocationally and in studying economic maladjustments.

8. Encourage local people of recognized social vision and forward-looking outlook to join the organization's board of directors and otherwise participate specifically in its program.

9. Strive to make the administrative operation of the organization itself conform to the kind of democratic and cooperative basis and method such as is being advocated in this study. Certainly, to make the structural and leadership patterns of one's own organization develop in ways believed to be an implementing of sound principles, is one of the most obvious and at the same time one of the most powerful object lessons which the organization can supply to its community. It is then in the wholesome position where it can truthfully and confidently say that it only suggests that other organizations (including the community as a whole in its local governance) try to interpret and apply the same *modus operandi* that is already established as a sound basis of control and operation in the organization itself. "Go thou and do likewise" is always one of the most effective appeals which can be made. Exhortation was, of course, never so powerful as example.

All of the foregoing are merely suggestions which the imaginative mind can enlarge upon in face-to-face contact with local conditions. If the obvious objection is offered that some or all of these suggestions may step on someone's toes, may frighten some of the community's "sacred cows," may involve taking a stand on an unpopular side, may frighten contributors, and the like, I can only say that any organization which knows what it stands for has to be prepared to stand for it at all costs or close up shop. "Woe unto you when all men speak well of you" was first said to a group of twelve men charged with the tremendous responsibility of proselyting for an unpopular and badly misunderstood cause, the strength of which has ever since only been truly advanced where the purity and austerity of its purpose have been kept inviolate.

There is, indeed, no escape from a dilemma here. Either the environing conditions of modern life help to advance "fellowship," or the "Kingdom of Heaven," or "personality growth," or whatever other phrasing one chooses in order to sloganize the devoted pursuit of the good life for all—or they do not. And if they do not, the mandate is upon organizations to see why they do not, how they do not, and how conditions can be modified in the desired direction. The conditions of a more abundant life no less than the will to a more abundant life have to be studied, understood, and striven for. "This ought ye to have done and not left the other undone" is a familiar way of reminding us of the bi-polar, interrelated fact about the mandate of our organizations.

There arises sooner or later, of course, the question as to what the organization may want to do in active effort to correct the conditions it finds and believes it knows the remedy for—at least in general terms. This problem of "direct action" is one to which different organizations are already supplying different answers. And it seems to me impossible to be dogmatic on this point. My own observations would frankly be somewhat cautionary, not for reasons of timidity, but for reasons of clarity about the function of the particular organization.

From the standpoint of program formulation, I believe certain cautions have to be stated. For example, none of the suggestions made above seems to me to imply any idea that all organizations *as such* should necessarily "go into politics," or in a certain sense "interfere in activities with which they have no concern"—

if by interference is meant direct, responsible organizational attack upon specific institutions or their shortcomings. The responsibility of a college or of a church is, of course, in this respect different from that of an organization striving in its community to sponsor social conditions which foster better living on the material side. Political alignment is one thing; agitation about and advocacy of specific reform measures is another. Political activity as such is for political parties, and for individuals and groups in their avowed political affiliations. But agitation for specific reforms related to the aim of the individual organization may well be an urgent mandate. A corrupt local government which is, for instance, obstructing some needed social change or protecting some festering local vice should challenge self-respecting citizens in many groups to act aggressively for correction.

Admittedly the line may in some cases seem to be drawn very fine. But the question of participation by the particular organization because of its concern over a given issue does not center about whether that issue is "political" or is "interference." It centers rather about *how that concern shall be manifested* once it is understood that the issue is one which creates adverse influences around the lives of members or of the community as a whole. And basically that concern would in the first instance seem to be one *of increasing understanding and of galvanizing the will to act once understanding is attained.* If after that point is reached the organization is convinced that it justifies itself only as it goes further into the arena of active support of public measures, then go it should, and having put its hand to the plow should not turn back.

This certainly is true: it is no longer (if it ever was) possible to hold in two dissociated compartments of living those acts which are "personal" and those which are "social." Personal action *is* social action. Social action is the action of persons. And there is no person apart from that person's action throughout the whole gamut of his activities. Nor is it possible in any conceivable way to divide personal action arbitrarily into "secular" and "religious." All actions are charged with religious significance when they represent a conscious devotion to some ideal end. Or they may not be so guided, in which case they represent a conscious or unconscious effort for satisfactions deemed purely personal and self-aggrandizing. Only the latter types of conduct are truly "secular." Apart from this there is no line to be drawn between those interests, problems, and concerns of individuals and of society which are or are not "religious" in implication. Every problem, every social, economic, or political issue which affects personality (and which does not?) has thus a "religious" bearing and burden.

Conscious and deliberate social change is brought about by "movements," by political parties, by pressure groups—in a word, by the effective mobilizing of public opinion. But movements, parties, and groups are composed of individuals—who are somewhat amenable to knowledge and definitely amenable to emotional loyalty to what they *believe* to be right. And the task of transmitting knowledge and creating the will to act—or active faith in something as true and right—is on the whole the field for organizations with subjective ends. And it is at their peril—at peril to their sole reason for survival—that they limit discussion or that they fail to have a clear, glowing, and confident vision of what they believe to be the right and righteousness for our day and age.

This, therefore, is my answer to the possible objection that the program suggestions here offered are subversive, dangerous, provocative, or irrelevant. "Pure religion and undefiled" is not jeopardized by treating every justifiable program activity as "religious." Only thus is the program given meaning and relevance in terms of current needs and perplexities. Only thus does the program come to grips with reality and get itself concerned with one of the two chief things that can and should concern it— namely, the assuring of ways of living, of institutional settings, which permit the human spirit a place in the sun where it can flower and fulfill itself.

49

I have said that the mandate of organizations with these subjective ends is to help forward *understanding* and to help *galvanize the individual will to act.*

The second of these aims centers about the dynamics of action. It is concerned with the arousing of the right kind of desire, the surcharging of the mind and heart with the right loyalties, the imparting or evoking of personal power to do good even when evil is tempting, and to have courage, faith, and devotion to carry on for high ends.

Here we are face to face with the deepest motives and mainsprings of action. Here if anywhere is where organizations rally their members out of confusion into unity of intention and integrity of vision and purpose; out of doubt and despair into faith and hope. Not that this central effort can be dissociated from organized concern for each individual's total social situation. But the emphasis in this connection is individual in focus.

I have no disposition to ignore this aspect of the problem. But it is, after all, not the major assignment of this study. I cannot refrain, however, from saying that where there is no real vision and passion and conviction, not only will there come no galvanizing of others but also there will come no truly profound understanding of the inwardness of the social or spiritual problems of our day. "This one thing *I know,*" has to be the ringing premise permeating all program activity. There *is* a faith which is at the heart of devotion, of sacrifice, and of victory. And it is only as that faith has possession of the leaders that works of value can result.

If leaders are bewildered or if appeals to the new generation seem lacking in persuasiveness, the fault may well be less in those appealed to than in the failure of the organization to know that it has a pearl of great price which it should sell all else to possess and to share.

Organizations require the sinews of war. And that means that individual donors or community chests have to be demonstrably convinced that a useful purpose is being served by the requesting organization. This is no place for an extended discussion of publicity methods.* But certain aspects of the public relations problem properly deserve mention against the background of what has gone before.

It may first be rightly assumed, I believe, that the relations with the board of directors should be such as to make it possible to utilize those relations in helpful ways direct and indirect with the larger public. "Names make news"; and whereas in the selection of boards this aspect should certainly not be the controlling one, it is important among others. The prestige value of the names of influential people on the board in getting money and moral support from others should not be ignored. With equal certainty it should be said that such influential people must be chosen in some relation to their personal outlooks and prejudices, and their known sympathy with the organization's real aims.

It is dangerous both to the institution and to its reputation in the community if the name and influence of some one prominent individual is allowed to become too dominant in its affairs. The very large donor, especially if on the board, can all too readily bring the organization under the public suspicion of being "kept," or at least of having an "angel." Increasingly, I believe, this type of support, which comes largely from one person or one corporation, is popularly suspected (whether justly or not is beside the point) as undemocratic, as illiberal, and as hazardous to the institution's autonomy and integrity of policy and growth. (It is the public relations aspect of this situation which I am primarily dwelling upon at the moment.) This condition is widely held to be contrary to the spirit of the times. A wide base for support and for self-support is urged as the only defensible alternative.

*Charles W. and Winona W. Gamble, *How to Raise Money* (New York, Association Press, 1943).

Public recognition of the value of the services rendered by an organization is admittedly essential to its esteem in the local community. Such recognition is by no means easy for organizations where subjective gains are the major aim. Often the direct and most impressive gains are not, cannot, and should not be made "news." And this being true, it is both permissible and desirable for the general executive to be mindful that occasionally events which do *dramatize* the institution's work should be held. Sheer *repetition* of public mention of the organization's name, personnel, and particular activities has of itself, apparently, considerable value as a prestige builder, and as a constant reminder throughout the community that something is happening in return for the donations or appropriations which have been made.

Surely it is prudent and canny for general executives (or someone) to know personally editors, reporters, news photographers, and feature article writers on the local papers. In fact, a similar friendly personal contact with other potential molders of local public opinion is desirable, including chamber of commerce secretaries, labor union executives, clergymen, and the like.

Without suggesting anything crass or blatant I do believe that the community should be allowed to know just as much, just as often, about what is happening, as possible. To give the impression of being "an up and coming organization" may seem to some executives a somewhat repellent task; but it is a logical and indispensable one under present conditions of the need for favorable community public opinion.

I am far from suggesting that organizations should be conducted "with an eye on the box office." But I am urging that the task of *interpreting* activities and results to the community through the board and through every other legitimate channel of public enlightenment available is a necessary one. Nor is it a question of "giving the public what it wants." It is a question of explaining again and again in the community *why* it is that the organization takes the stand and pursues the line that it does. It is as important that motives be clarified as it is that methods be explained. It is a question also of showing the supporting public that *what the organization knows it wants and is working for in high and serene confidence will prove to be of value to the community.* The transmission of that conviction to local supporters is the essence of the public relations program.

STAFF MEMBERS AS INDIVIDUALS IN THE COMMUNITY

Some will say that I have temporized in discussing the amount of "direct action" which the organizations here under discussion can wisely take. And it should naturally be true that many staff workers and many members will be anxious *as individuals* to take a stand for or to participate in movements for social betterment to which their organizations are not directly committed.

It is for this reason that I venture to add a few hints about a program for the individual, since the query, "What can I do about this personally?" is so often asked. There is no pretense of completeness about the following suggestions; but they may serve as a stimulus to further individual exploration:

1. The individual should be sure that he exercises his franchise so as to vote for the political party he believes to be most in harmony with what he himself sees as desirable political objectives.

2. He should support specific legislation which he believes in by communicating his convictions to the proper legislators.

3. He should support by voluntary contributions or by avocational volunteer activity, or both, the efforts of specific *ad hoc* organizations, local and national, devoted to the forwarding of aims he believes in. (There are increasing numbers of these, and thus an increasing chance "to be counted" and to be vocal vicariously in support of divers good causes.)

4. He should keep himself informed of current affairs by a careful selection of newspapers, periodicals, and books. Nothing less than a serious plan in this matter is his mandate as a conscientious citizen.

5. He should as far as possible in his role as consumer and as investor try to support enterprises and policies he believes to be sound.

53

6. He should, where his views on relevant issues are sought or expected in organizations to which he belongs, "testify to the faith that is in him," in giving persuasive support to the stand he takes.

7. He should try to get his own personal satisfaction and sense of duty done out of his persuasiveness, and not out of a dramatic, absolute, and inappropriately timed stridency in affronting people who disagree with him, or out of efforts to shock them. He will use a teaching sense in his effort to bear witness to the truth—not be a bull in a china shop. There is a time for all things, but the basis on which to decide *what* thing, is normally a question of what will be most effective in influencing others in the direction one believes they should take. This is in some part a matter of vocabulary, of using idioms that people are familiar with; and of starting with the preconceptions which people have. No one group in the community, for example, has a monopoly upon the Constitution, or "democracy," or "liberty."

8. He should try in the organization with which he is vocationally associated to use his influence to see that the organization itself—in whole or in the part where he has power and scope—begins to operate on principles which harmonize with his basic views of the proper relation of structure to attitude and of good will to good methods (see the entire study above for the further definition of this). Here, it would seem, is one of the most direct mandates imposed upon us, because here is an opportunity which comes definitely in the direct conduct of one's own familiar work situation. Without necessarily being a gadfly on the back of the organization, one can surely exert tactfully an influence for betterment in this field of building cooperativeness.

In general, it may be concluded on this point that, if it be agreed that we live in an age of rather acute social and economic transition, the individual's responsibility is to try, in so far as lies in his power, to see that the transition proceeds with a minimum of personal ill will, of acrimonious conflicts, of unwarranted allegations of personal wilfulness against members of other groups in society with whom one may disagree. The times do not call for bitterness, hatred, and despair; they call for insight, for the encouraging of fraternal attitudes, and for hopefulness and faith in betterment. The measure of one's stand for the good life lies in this: that one helps to conserve those values historically proved to be good and strives eagerly to develop as good those newer values of cooperativeness, a sense of collective responsibility and institutional unity, which have become as never before the conditions of personal well-being in a highly organized and interrelated society.

One thing is certain. To decide to do nothing, to carry on as at present, because one does not know what to do (individually or in respect to one's organization) is no answer. Thus not to act is the unforgivable sin of *omission,* which can be far more subtly dangerous and corroding to the spirit than the usual decalogue of sins of commission. The time has come when "to take a stand" is necessary. And if taking a stand is dangerous or is difficult, it matters not. It always has been in any cause worthy of the name. Better far to go down fighting for the truth as one sees it than to carry on a living death—either the person or the institution standing only as an empty shell to remind us that once some now outdated purpose there stood enshrined!

CONCLUSION

If it be thought that this discussion has been a strange mixture of ideas—ideas about purposes, organization policies, working methods, personal obligations—all stirred up together and *not* sweetened to suit the reader's taste, that impression may be unavoidable. But the mixture and the juxtaposition of ideas are deliberate. Indeed, my whole theme has been that organizations embody and reflect the purposes and ideas of their leaders and members, that organization aims do not exist and do not get served apart from the tangible working methods and organized structure of human relations within that organization.

The time has come to see the objectives and functionings of people in associations as two inseparable halves of one fact: that of an organization pursuing its aims with methods consistent with those aims. If these two—objectives and functionings—hang together with an observable and logical inner unity and consistency, the organization can generate untold power and influence. If these two are at odds and are obviously inconsistent, there exists a central weakness which saps the vitality of the organism and eventually places it on the defensive.

In an hour when social, economic, political, and moral values seem shifting and uncertain, the imperative is greater than ever upon organizations with subjective ends to know what they stand for and whether what they do and how they do it squares with their professed aims. And what these organizations profess to stand for does require that they give at once some earnest scrutiny and constructive reconsideration to how they are organized, controlled, and operated, in order to be sure that a true consistency of pattern and unity of working drive are present.

The implementing of fellowship requires a fresh examination of structure. The objectifying of good will requires a rethinking of good methods. The realizing of the good life can take place only as associated action expresses itself through good organizations.

PART II

DEMOCRACY IN ADMINISTRATION*

Look with me in imagination at the life and the work of a mail sorter in the Post Office Department, a file clerk in the Federal Civil Service Commission, a cable splicer in the New England Telephone and Telegraph Company, a grade school teacher in Harlem, a foundry helper in a plant of the United States Steel Corporation, a sales clerk in the A. & P., a seaman on a tanker of the Standard Oil Company.

All these present to those concerned with the quality of the good life for all persons in a democracy, a common problem. That problem is: how shall individuals feel and know that they are real, growing, thriving persons who can call their souls their own as they plod on through the day's work? How can personality be fulfilled in and through the tasks of modern large-scale agencies—corporate or public? How, in more abstract terms, are personal freedom and economic productivity reconciled in today's society?

Put in other words, I ask how we propose to face up in a democracy to conflicts of group interests and blocs, to a growing sense of bureaucratic stultifications, to the need for stimulating in all individuals initiative and creative zest up to the top of their powers? Again, I ask how do we prevent the usurping of social power (economic, political, educational, or other) by those with overdeveloped power lusts? How do we face up to the tardiness of legislative bodies in laying down the just and necessary rules of orderly human relations? How do we overcome the false belief that corporate groups by pursuing their own self-interests are somehow automatically advancing the interests of us all?

---

* This Part was originally delivered as a lecture before the Institute for Religious Studies, New York City.

What is needed for clarification here, I suggest, is a clearer notion of the inwardness of the democratic idea—a more radical probing of its deeper realities and implications, and a careful scrutiny of the fundamental meanings centering around the idea of administration.

We live in what we claim to be a democratic society. We operate in many walks of life through organized procedures which are administrative in character. And somehow these two big ideas have to be brought into some defensible working relation. Or, on the other hand, they have no such relation and should each go its own way. But that they have an organic working relation will be my thesis.

The pattern of the argument will unfold as follows: What is democracy? What is the democratic process? What relation to it have the ideas of science, of leadership, and of human affection? In the light of answers to these questions, I shall consider what administration is and how it operates; I shall define democratic administration and characterize its implications. Certain cautions will then be suggested as to popular misconceptions of the application of democratic thinking to administrative action. I return at the end to the human persons with whom a democracy is concerned, in order to point the way in which administration in its properly conceived operation helps to bring a measure of personal salvation through collaborative participation.

DEMOCRACY DEFINED

Democracy has high in its constituent elements the aim of conserving and enhancing the personality of all individuals,—the idea of respect for the integrity of the person and of the primary value of developing persons as worthy and worthful ends in themselves. Yet this proposition depends for its acceptance upon the meaning which is read into the word "personality." I take it that this includes the discovery and use of unique talents, the fullest possible expression of creative powers, the responsible assumption of a share in shaping the conditions which are found to make growth in the quality of personal living possible. The idea of personality includes also the acquiring of sufficient knowledge and understanding, the sense of enough status with one's peers, the sentiment of friendly attachment with one's fellows, the possession of enough voice and power in one's society, so that one feels that he is in fact helping to shape the conditions which make possible the achievement of individual, creative release. It has to do also with a continuing reexamination of self and society to assure that the dignity of the person is being maintained under changing conditions.

The growth mentioned here is not undirected. It is looking inward to disciplined control and fruition of productive ability. It is looking outward to that surrounding environment that will invite personal contribution, allow criticism, and hopefully support the long-time creative urges of many persons.

Personality seen as an end requires complementary and supplementary support in community terms. We are thus concerned also, as an end, with a shared companionship of rich personalities who are seeking to live "the good life" in an unlimited and beloved community. The words "unlimited" and "beloved" are endowed with a special significance which I do not here expatiate upon but which are meant to suggest both a universal and a fraternal regard and sentiment. Today we do not have complete agreement as to whether that community is to be characterized as a Kingdom of God or a Kingdom of Man. But I have a notion that the enlightened protagonists of both Kingdoms are nearer together in their allegiances than they sometimes assume.

I do conclude, for myself, that loyalty to the Kingdom which is becoming is an absolute claim made upon us. We deny it at our peril. We repudiate it, and we are at once in a morass of moral irresponsibility and futility. Surely whatever of civilization the world achieves is rooted in the absolute hold this allegiance has upon us. We are absolutely obligated to realize through the growing personalities of all a commonly operated society which will be fraternal in aim and method. That, at least, will be the premise here. If personality in a community with fraternal sentiments has some definiteness as a major democratic end—if this defines to a considerable degree the nature of democracy— we have next to inquire what processes of social relation minister to personal growth and in what climate of sentiment that growth is most assuredly fostered.

The Democratic Process

The democratic process can now be measurably identified by the use it uniquely makes of the following succession of steps: (a) You define your constituency (you establish the fact of citizenship or membership); (b) you identify what groupings or breakdowns seem logically and conveniently to appear within your constituency as a basis for representing special points of view when common issues are under discussion (typically in political affairs these groupings have been geographic even within the town meeting); (c) you identify, articulate and represent these exigent interests; (d) you create a continuing body where representative deliberation shall take place; (e) you assure regular deliberation; (f) you try to supply such leadership to the deliberative process as will press the group toward clear and sound agreements; (g) you try to supply the conferees with the fullest possible measure of facts relevant to the issues under discussion; (h) you reach agreements with as little affront to the good will of the momentary minority as possible; (i) you try out the solution (in politics it is usually new legislation) and see how it works; (j) you review in some manner from time to time how salutary the solution is in action, and how satisfactory the leadership is in purposive and personal terms.

In this democratic process the associated persons explicitly place themselves in a relation of reciprocal obligation to their fellows. And they do this, at least ideally, in an absolute and unequivocal way. It is true and right that they want some things for themselves and for their constituents out of democratic group

60

action. Certain self-interests have to be served, and these basically relate to certain phases of personality fulfillment. But also a constituency has to come to agreements upon matters other than closely personal ones which affect and advance a more general welfare. Devotion to self-fulfillment and to social helpfulness do thus in some measure get practical reconciliation. A certain reciprocal benefit usually arises out of this shared effort to handle common problems. The process is not perfect. But it is educational in the sense that the vision of each participant as to what is the good for self and for society is widened. And an operating test is made which is educational, and which is also subject to correction if a proposal is tried and found wanting.

What we are thus in process of achieving is a necessary, prudent, and productive sharing of power, of knowledge, and of respect.* And irrespective of methods conventionally thought to be "democratic," such as voting and the like, wherever sharing on all these fronts goes forward, where creative release of persons is taking place, where responsibility for achieving these aims is being equally shared—*there is democracy*. And the methods which eventuate to do all this successfully *are* democratic. And they are absolutely imposed once the end in view is agreed to.

In short, democracy works out its destinies by a body of methods which have a certain practical and tested validity. The soundness of the results and the wisdom of the agreement depend, however, upon the competence with which the successive steps are taken. For present purposes I allude further to only two of these—namely, the need for facts and the analysis of problems as a basis for enlightened agreements; and the importance of a dynamic leadership to spur us toward willing agreements and equally to help us to discern through the facts the sound hypotheses to follow.

---

* See "Legal Education and Public Policy: Professional Training in the Public Interest," by H. D. Lasswell and M. S. McDougal, *Yale Law Journal* (March, 1943), p. 217.

The need for facts and for analyisis is the need for science, and at this point historically viewed a weak link in the chain confronts us. The weakness has to do with a democracy's slowness in acknowledging the need for accurate grasp of its problems, persistence in finding the relevant data, willingness promptly to accept the indicated solutions. But eventually democracy does test. It tests against its own inner goals; and if necessary it changes its programs.

Science also tests by definition, but with what criteria as to soundness of outcome in the social areas of exploration depends upon its linkage to democracy. Indeed, we see today that the very freedom of science to pursue its inquiries relentlessly and disinterestedly requires a reasonably free society in which to function. We are also coming slowly to see that scientific method suitably adapted to social subject matter promises to yield us practical proofs that the ends and processes of democracy are intrinsically valuable. Moreover, science surely promises a vast illumination as to ways of assuring democratic gains by the discovery of many of the conditions of personality fulfillment. Do you want longevity? Do you want adequate sustenance for all the people? Do you want freedom from anxiety and neurosis? Do you want trained minds and disciplined judgments? Do you want conflicts over territory or racial status minimized? Do you want workers in industry as partners rather than as indifferent drudges? These are democratic hopes. They are also scientific problems. That administration is honeycombed with its problems to be solved only by scientific effort I shall later emphasize.

The method of science is inherently a self-correcting method.* The element of corroborative test is always present; and success is in relation to an end sought or a new hypothesis reached. Is it true to observable experience, and does it give an answer which is useful in the premises? These are criteria we

---

* See "Ethical Objectivity Through Science," by H. S. Fries, *Philosophical Review* (November, 1943).

ask scientific inquiry to satisfy. In the physical sciences these criteria are more readily satisfied than in the social sciences. For in the latter we have always to ask: where do we look for the facts; who has them; of what essence are they (psychological, biological, sociological, etc.); how can we be sure our proposed solution is sound; who is willing to give it a trial; and, crucial beyond all else, what is the measure of success?

The process of operation in science is now familiar. The steps in the scientific method I mention only because of the light they throw upon its relation of the process of democracy. The steps are clear: identification of the problem to be solved, probing of its every element and factor, examination of the interrelations and connections among the parts looking for clues toward the answer, efforts to state a hypothesis or solution, testing the solution to be sure that it works.

The scientist places himself in an absolute sense responsibly under the obligation of truth seeking, of subordination of self to objectivity—or, with equal truth, the obligation of finding self-fulfillment through obedience to processes which make possible the discovery of natural or social law. How the scientist applies the laws he discovers depends at bottom upon the kind of society in which he lives. His contribution is thus as dependent upon his social setting as is his very freedom of inquiry. And again we remind ourselves that the obligation to be scientific is absolute.

Beyond Group Conflicts

It is next important to make more explicit how a democracy comes to reach the numerous agreements upon which common aims and common programs depend. Even on those issues as to which scientists can offer evidence as leading to a sound answer (as, for example, the methods to abate the spread of a disease) there has to be public acceptance of their findings. And there are many other problems (as, for example, the division of the social income) which scientifically speaking yield no absolutely sound answers. To resolve conflicts is thus crucial in a democracy; for it is assumed by definition that issues in conflict are not to be decided by violence, or by the destruction of dissident factions, or by enslaving them to some dominant social power.

Democracy seeks a dynamic unity of disposition about the ways of conducting itself. Hence it seeks loyalty to shared companionship. It seeks good will toward other men. It seeks, if you please, affection or love as a warm sentiment of solicitude and deep concern for understanding harmony among members of a common society. Actually it finds its processes blocked and resisted by special group interests. And as the technological and organizational aspects of life increase in sheer size and complexity, this problem takes on new urgency. And the solution of it requires great strength and wisdom of social leadership and great strength of affectionate sentiment among men to offset the tensions which are in fact created. For the special group interests— whether they be named as "pressure groups" or more accurately as "functional groups"—are in action partial and fragmented in the ends they seek. They are sorely tempted to see the welfare —and usually the material welfare—of the group interest as more important than and superior to the common welfare. And the question is: can a democracy invoke a community interest as controlling over special interests? How does a democracy demonstrate that personality is not fulfilled apart from the whole group of persons implicated? In other words, the root question here becomes—how can people be led to place a high value on widened interests and concerns (both as to time and place)? And unless I am gravely mistaken, this question means—how can we be led to give effect in individual conduct to what has historically been called a law of love?

THE PLACE OF A LAW OF LOVE

The answer parallels that given in looking at the processes of democracy and of science. Love in its personal phases and unity among men in its social phases requires: (a) identification of and focus upon those to be loved; (b) understanding of their desires and needs at their best; (c) disposition to take those desires and needs intelligently into account as factors in the social equation to be solved; (d) action directed to including in its planning the facts about the loved ones and their fulfillment; (e) the practical manifestation of informed behavior calculated to bring about a loving response, that is, an agreeing and a cooperative response. The agreement and the cooperation will arise from the tangible evidences of concern which the new plan of corporate action and the human attitude of love naturally evoke. And this fraternal attitude, we further remind ourselves, assumes equality of treatment and freedom of opportunity among the persons involved in respect to their choices in behavior.

In love, as in democracy and in science, the effective basic devotion is directed outward, away from the individual self to other selves. The degree of intelligent selflessness marks the degree of loving concern. The welfare of the beloved is a norm for the relevant behavior of the lover. The recourse, when necessary, to self-sacrifice, to giving up one's life for the end in view, to absolute devotion, is an experienced reality when democracy or science or human affection are witnessed at their most exalted. Once again, within this total frame the obligation of a law of love is absolute.

What bearing, now, has this need for the active influence in human motives for a law of love upon the uses of leadership and upon the removal of social conflicts of group interest? It has this relation—it reminds us that the successful conditions of human cooperation require the example, the stimulus, the guidance, and the vitalizing of leaders. He who loves me, let him take up his cross and follow me—this is a universal prescription for the drawing out of love and loyalty. It has a personalized origin; it gets its power through the suggestion of and the emulation of loving persons. The good leader loves the led and in so doing he calls forth loving behavior of the led in the directions which he suggests. The good leader is doing unto others what he would that they should do were they in his place. And thus he secures the desired response that the led shall widen the area of their loving and interested concern.

The leaders are thus the ones that a democracy looks to in order to make sure not only that rightful group self-interests are served but even more that the relation of such interests to broader interests is grasped, and that group interests have properly and wisely been subordinated to a larger community welfare. And this subordination has to take place not grudgingly but willingly, and with a genuine sense on the part of all the followers, of the felicity of the larger view and the wider responsibility entailed. Such felicity is but another way of identifying a loving sentiment and motive.

THE INTERPRETATION OF DEMOCRACY, SCIENCE, AND LOVE

My analysis has now reached a point where, before going on to discuss administration, a summarizing of certain phases of the argument will high-light the developing thesis. Democracy, science, love—each works itself into the realities of overt action in analogous and parallel ways. The similarities of operational method here are revealing. For in each of the three processes of human action we seek to define areas of concern, problem, and difficulty; we probe to grasp factual realities; we seek clues as to how to resolve tensions without violence and organize together seemingly incompatible or unrelated facts, forces, and persons; we find a likely basis for action—a formula or principle which gives a new operating pattern; we act, and we appraise how it works. And that we *should* so act, seems an imperative required by the nature of the task which inevitably has to be assumed when democrats are true to themselves, when scientists are true to their commitment, and when lovers (in the broader sense) are true to those whom they love. We have democracy, science, or affection in effective working action on no other basis.

Surely it is not accidental that this kind of process chain illuminates and assists in our search for ends and for means, for values and for ways of strengthening those values. The way of life and the ways to set our feet on that way here come through to some broad coherence and to some rational and defensible direction. In short, to act democratically we act with knowledge and we act with love. And so to act is a moral imperative, inescapable if there is to be fulfillment of any of these three instrumentalities to the creation of a Kingdom of Righteousness. Are we therefore wrong in concluding that this intertwining of commitments is essentially an *absolute* claim upon us?

ADMINISTRATION DEFINED

It is only in the light of all this that we can look with any discernment upon that subdivision of human conduct to which the name "administration" is given. I call you back at this point to the individuals imaginatively mentioned in my first paragraph. I remind you that personal freedom and fulfillment in serviceable organizations are our central problem.

What then is administration? Brooke Adams (in *The Theory and Social Revolution,* pp. 207-8) suggests its comprehensive meaning. He says: "Administration is the capacity to coordinate many, and often conflicting, social energies in a single organism, so adroitly that they shall operate as a unity." Again, he says: "Administration or generalization is not only the faculty upon which social stability rests, but is, possibly, the highest faculty of the human mind."

Operationally, administration is the process and agency which lays down the broad object for which an organization and its management are to strive, which establishes the broad policies under which they are to operate, and which gives general oversight to the continuing effectiveness of the total organization in reaching the objective sought.

A further sense in which the word is used is important to mention. In our American political democracy and, growing in part out of what was in the eighteenth century believed to be a necessary corollary of it, we have proceeded on the assumption

67

of the need for "checks and balances." The executive branch of public power was to be checked by the legislative and both were to be checked by the judicial arm. Today a vast new fourth function of bodies of public administration has developed. These have been found necessary to carry on the public business. At the Federal level alone before the war these agencies employed between one and two million public servants. In private corporate life similarly we have single companies employing the tens of thousands of people. All of this gives rise to problems of administrative powers, laws, regulations, human relations, incentives, cooperation, and loyalties.

Shall the relation of person to person, of group to group, of different administrative levels in the operating hierarchy to one another, be controlled by the familiar military pattern of authority or not? And if not, what substitutes are available and how do we work them?

The Process of Administration

Answers to these questions begin to be suggested if we examine even briefly what goes on when administration is in action. If administration has to do in a primary way with the purpose of the organization, I believe it is justifiable to start with two assertions: first, that indoctrination in purpose throughout the organization is an obvious need from the point of view of high morale; and, second, that organization purpose is at bottom never completely single. I shall not here elaborate the first point, which at least in theory is now widely accepted. As to the second, for whatever overt and obvious purpose a group is brought together, it remains constantly true that the membership, clientele, or so-called employee portion of the group has to be kept implicated enough to feel somewhat happy and satisfied as *persons* in the process of acting for that purpose. Hence the supplementary purpose of being mindful to keep the people tied in is always integral. How far this implies their fulfillment and how far it means their self-effacement depends on many factors. Even Hitler found both the

68

illusion of participation and the indoctrination of "joy through self-abnegation" to be necessary parts of his purpose program.

Keeping the whole group in line and in loyalty thus demands an attitude of solicitude on the part of the administrator. He had better be not only attentive to distress signals but affirmatively eager to make it clear in action that *persons* and their satisfactions are being reckoned with as well as company purposes and their attainment. He, after all, broadly initiates the ongoing of the enterprise. He wants a good response; he should be anxious that down from the top a sense of responsible concern is felt and that up from the bottom a wide human support is forthcoming. In other words good administration requires good communication growing out of good attitude. And this *must* start with the executive as leader. Communication, moreover, is successful only when it is intelligible, when it commends itself to agreement, when it is unrestrained, spontaneous and thus creative, and when finally it is subject to comeback or criticism. It has in consequence to embrace discussion and face-to-face conference and not just telling by one to another. In good administration communication is full, free, fair, and up as well as down. And the reason for the communication, let us be clear, is, first, to interpret persuasively the group purpose to be served and, second, to keep in proper view the welfare of the associated persons as the condition of their going all out for their associated purposes. Mr. Jack speaking over the amplifier to his employees at Jack and Heintz and John Mason Brown broadcasting from the bridge to the men below decks on his war craft—these are instances of communication related to purpose, to good management, and to shared personal commitment.

Again, no astute administrator will ignore the leadership phases of his task. Someone must supply the "oomp," the vitalizing, the charging of the individual batteries which together run the total dynamo of the organization. Someone has to symbolize the Big Idea and personalize the Main Drive. Someone rescues the individuals involved from too great self-interest and self-centeredness. We all tacitly ask to be saved from our little selves into our large selves and loyalties. "He redeemeth our life from destruction" is the deeper achievement of the leader. Self-transcendence and self-fulfillment are reconciled where the leadership role has done its finest work.

Finally, administration as leadership gets agreement and cooperative action which is more than perfunctory and becomes eagerly creative where responsibility is first clearly defined but, even more important, is explicitly shared. It has to be shared, in fact, for the labors of many are required. It better be shared in eagerness by executives as the key to the desired creative response. And the executive is wise who invites it. The only practical questions here are—shared to what degree and with what success? Success depends upon a *complete* sharing of all knowledge of relevant facts. The power to issue decisions may be and should be unitary; but decisions arise out of confronting the total fact realities and from judgment gained by immersion in concrete experiences which are occurring far away from the administrator's desk. To share responsibility is at bottom to share knowledge. Secondarily, it is to share desire to profit by the facts in wiser action. Hence to give facts and to receive facts, these are both imperatives.

Knowledge, unity of purpose, vigor of desire—these in the long run all prosper together. Kept separate they wilt and evaporate. The drive or dynamic to much effortful action for the individual is to want to do something personally felt to be important, through the channel of group efforts known to be contributing to the common end. This is only one of numerous reasons why administrators *have* to be experts in the dynamics of human nature at its affirmative and creative best.

GOOD ADMINISTRATION AS DEMOCRATIC

But what now—even with this quick look at administration —have we been saying? I believe all of these, as characteristic aspects of administration, add up to the view that at its dynamic

70

best administration includes the task of personality creation. Administration in its wisest manifestations makes an appeal to wider, less selfish loyalties, to fuller creative release, to broader knowledge and agreement to purpose, method, and fact, to cooperative, associated, responsible conduct in and through which individuals find themselves redeemed—brought to meaningful life and endeavor through an associated effort. And what is all this but democratic fulfillment? What is all this but a resolute pursuit of scientific method in order to possess the rational conditions of adequate control, accurate prediction, group mastery, and devotion to a defined end? What is all this but a widening and generalizing of affectionate concern or informed love showing itself in a specific organized setting?

The conditions of good administration,—in quality and meaning of purpose, in human attitudes, in powers of communication and opportunities for criticism, in the inwardness of leadership responsibilities entailed, in the distribution of responsibility and of knowledge,—these conditions are *democratic* conditions.

We thus come to a conception of administration which is not wishful, is not a mere juggling of pleasant words, is not an impossible or idealistic claim. It has operative suggestiveness and fruitfulness. We come to a sense of the inwardness of administration which takes account of our understanding of human nature, of social organizations, and of the productive interpenetration of the two. We come to a grasp of administration which has operational validity in relation to the kind of democratic, scientific, and personal ends we have found to be worthy. We come to a conception which imposes a moral imperative upon those who administer. We come, in short, to a conception which is rightfully named democratic administration—a conception *absolutely* implicit for the fulfillment of a democratic society.

DEMOCRATIC ADMINISTRATION DEFINED AND APPLIED

Democratic administration is thus definable as that overall direction of an organization which assures that purposes and policies are shared in the making, that methods are understood and agreed to, that individual potentialities are being enhanced, that corporate or group ends are being realized with a maximum of release of shared creative power and a minimum of human friction. It implies further a periodic, orderly, cooperative review of total performance, of leadership in action, of effectiveness of method at every point. It brings to pass collaboration as willing, coordination as informed and continuing, personality growth as an actuality and a continuing promise.

Much should be added to fill out the implications of such a definition. Two or three points only will be selected. I mention, first, the body of thought centering around Professor James Burnham's concept of a "managerial revolution" and the rise of a managerial elite which would be the responsible new aristocracy of tomorrow's world. He proposes a new caste system, an alignment of the forces of society as between ruling brains and ruled brawn, between thinkers and doers, between power-holders and power-followers. But actually here is complete disregard of the true conditions of social stability, which include elevation of persons through their creative sharing of responsibility, the generating from within individuals of their desires for growth, for larger fulfillment, and for self-transcendence. Burnham's thesis has a plausible popularity for those now in the seats of economic and administrative power. But it is based on a false psychology and a specious and spiritually impoverished notion of the ways toward a shared companionship in a wider human community. In short, it is dangerous doctrine—subversive, retrogressive, and spiritually stultifying.

Rather, in complete contrast to this concept, I offer the opposite alternative—and I do so with affirmative confidence and moral enthusiasm, and with an urgent plea that a democracy *must* by its inevitable inner impulsion move toward some such alternative as this, both negatively as the price of its survival and positively as the way of life which it inherently implies. This other alternative is to know that we seek to build within a democratic

72

political society and subordinate to it a group of constitutional governments of economic units by industries, by functions, by large administrative responsibilities. And these governments are to be comprised of an inclusive, rank-and-file citizenship. The task of that citizenship from top management to humblest porter is to create and to operate the functional agency as a responsible and accountable arm of the body politic.*

In these respective administrative areas we are to create and operate under constitutional forms not merely as a measure of prudence, expediency, or efficiency at the level of material gain— but because to develop citizenship in our economic and administrative substates is *the* condition of assuring that the conduct of these states-within-the-state will work approximately in the public interest, in the interest of personality fulfillment, in the interest of democratic aspiration and method consistently flowering in *all* branches of our common life. It is in this direction too (with the truly democratic planning that it can imply) that we may look for a resolution of the dilemma between profit-motivated policies of restricted output and those of high employment with high-level distribution of consumer purchasing power combined with low unit costs.

If in particulars this alternative seems unattractive I say only that the principle has to be affirmed (let the details be what they will) that democratic procedures of sorts will not only "work," but that we are committed to them by our growing awareness as to where and how it is possible to give substance to the precious values which it is our destiny here on earth to catch down into human realization.

In passing let me say that there are aspects of what is loosely called the "corporative state," as Catholic thinkers have long recognized, which organizationally have much to commend them in a society of large-scale administration, production, and trade.

---

* This idea is more fully developed in Chapter XIV on "The Industry Unit as a Democratic Instrument," in my *New Adventures in Democracy* (New York, McGraw-Hill Book Co., 1939).

All that we have to do is to move into this area of corporative organization with the idea of universal, democratic, economic citizenship under constitutional government as the basic premise of our effort, our structure, and our motive. We cannot—we could not if we would—abandon the task of the administration of the instruments of control and of production on a huge scale. The international cartel is but one illustration of the most recent extension in scale here. But what we can and must do—by the democratic approach of representation of vital interests, formal consent, shared knowledge, periodic review of executive action, and all the rest—is to build into our economic, governmental, and other social agencies those constitutional provisions which bring citizen participation and bring citizen freedom at the price it has always cost—at the price of eternal shared vigilance and responsibility for ultimate control through organized, individual creative expression.*

MISUNDERSTANDINGS OF DEMOCRATIC ADMINISTRATION

In conclusion let me suggest some of the things which democracy in administration does *not* mean and does *not* have to imply if we stick to fundamentals, use our heads creatively, and are inventive about new social mechanisms.

The infusion of democratic concern into administration does not necessarily mean adherence to the present notions of checks and balances. It does not mean wide, general voting on all sorts of operating and technical issues. It does not mean the inevitable growth of a bi-party or multi-party system to aggravate sharp alignments on issues of administrative policy. It does not mean that at numerous levels of administrative action, the administra-

---

* It is at this point and in this manner that we are able constructively, sensibly, and democratically to meet the contentions of men like Von Mises, in his *Omnipotent Government*, and Hayek, in his *The Road to Serfdom,* who are claiming that genuine freedom is not to be found in the necessary collaborative agencies of the great society, unless we return to or advance to "free competition" and small-scale operation.

tor shall be elected by those whose work he oversees. The election of direct work supervisors by those supervised seems rarely to have proved effective. It does not mean that in committees we talk ourselves into inaction because talk is easier than actual productive work—although this is a genuine hazard to be guarded against.

Democratic administration *does* mean a clear distinction between policy making and policy execution. It means that the process of determining purpose, policy, and method is advisedly seen as shared, and the process of oversight and direction is seen as unified and single.

It means, also, that in practice by shared responsibility and explicit common participation in defining aims and processes and in appraising outcomes, we reconcile freedom and organization, personality and corporate loyalty. It means that personal creativity flows into group achievement; and personal enlargement and security in affection are attained in cooperative labors where the full capacities of individuals are called forth and are rewarded.

The Thesis Summarized

What, it seems to me, we have arrived at is an examination of facts and forces, and influences inner and outer in our social life, which gives them organic relation, rational clarity, and scientifically based validation. How human nature is known and stirred, how individuals and groups are led, how scientific advances are utilized, how personality values are strengthened, how institutional structures are built as democratic, how an enlightened loving attitude can permeate human relations without weakening the fabric of group discipline—it is this complex of human realities we have been probing and integrating.

Recall that at the outset we asked how the generality of men and women in the run-of-mill tasks of daily life in our great society are to get the necessary sense that they are persons and that life ministers to their pursuit of happiness.

For myself I am led to conclude that in and through their work relations is one valid approach to the way in which human lives are served by serving. Democracy in administration is not a quixotic phrase. It is that total arrangement and interplay of human relationships in specific institutional groups, which alone can satisfy the terms of the equation here posed for solution. Democratic administration is at once the setting, the plot, and the acting out of a drama which we are imperatively required to perform in order to give living actuality to these basic values and ends of the human enterprise.

RELATED PUBLICATIONS

Baxter, Bernice, and Cassidy, Rosalind. *Group Experience—The Democratic Way.* Harper and Brothers, New York. $2.50.

Beavers, Helen D. *Administration in the YWCA: Principles and Procedures.* Woman's Press, New York. 75¢.

Bowman, LeRoy C. *How to Lead Discussions.* Woman's Press, New York. 35¢.

de Huszar, George B. *Practical Applications of Democracy.* Harper and Brothers, New York. $2.00.

Fortson, John L. *How to Make Friends for Your Church.* Association Press, New York. $2.00.

Ingels, Belle. *Administration in the YWCA: Planning.* Woman's Press, New York. 50¢.

Lies, Eugene T. *How You Can Make Democracy Work.* Association Press, New York. $1.75.

Lippitt, Lucile. *Committee Cues.* 25¢.

McCandless, James W. *Prediction, Planning and Control.* Association Press, New York. $1.00.

McCandless, James W. and G. S. Bilheimer, Editors. *Handbook of Association Business Administration.* Association Press, New York. $3.00.

Metcalf, Henry C., and Urwick, L. *Dynamic Administration—The Collected Paper of Mary Parker Follett.* Harper and Brothers, New York. $3.50.

O'Shaughnessy, Michael. *Economic Democracy and Private Enterprise.* Harper & Brothers, New York. $2.00.

Russ, Marie. *Administration in the YWCA: The Electorate.* Woman's Press, New York. 50¢.

77

Shafer, H. M. *Principles of Democratic Personnel Relationships in Administration* (Pamphlet). School of Education, University of Oregon, Eugene, Oregon. 50¢.

Sims, Mary S. *The Natural History of a Social Institution—the Y.W.C.A.* Woman's Press, New York. $1.50.

Swift, Arthur L. *Make Your Agency More Effective.* Association Press, New York. $3.00.

Tead, Ordway. *The Art of Leadership.* McGraw-Hill Book Company, New York. $2.50.

Tead, Ordway. *Human Nature and Management.* McGraw-Hill Book Company, New York. $3.50.

Tead, Ordway. *The Importance of Administration in International Action.* Carnegie Endowment for International Peace, New York. Bulletin No. 407. 5¢.

Tead, Ordway. *New Adventures in Democracy.* Harper and Brothers, New York. $2.50.

Teall, Briseis. *Administration in the YWCA: Staff Supervision.* Woman's Press, New York. 50¢.

Urice, Jay. *Working Together.* Association Press, New York. 25¢.